MW01046157

Being and Becoming

In Search of a Positive World

Paul Corke

Bloomington, IN Milton Keynes, UK

authorHOUSE

AuthorHouse™
1663 Liberty Drive, Suite 200
Bloomington, IN 47403
www.authorhouse.com
Phone: 1-800-839-8640

AuthorHouse™ UK Ltd.
500 Avebury Boulevard
Central Milton Keynes, MK9 2BE
www.authorhouse.co.uk
Phone: 08001974150

© 2006 Paul Corke. All rights reserved.

No part of this book may be reproduced, stored in a retrieval system, or transmitted by any means without the written permission of the author.

First published by AuthorHouse 7/6/2006

ISBN: 1-4259-3979-1 (sc)

Printed in the United States of America
Bloomington, Indiana

This book is printed on acid-free paper.

Introduction

Being and Becoming. In Search of a Positive World. You've read self-development books before. You know the kind of thing to expect. Well, put your helmet on and fasten your seatbelt because you are in for a real rollercoaster of a ride with this one!

Paul Corke has based this book on the question: *What motivates man to live?* And yes, it explores what motivation is, how to identify what really motivates us, and how to stay self motivated. What is the ultimate motivation that drives us all to live, and how can we use this knowledge to become and be all we were meant to be?

It's more than that though, much more. Paul takes his reader on an amazing journey: a trip through past, present, and future; an exploration of what has been, what is, and what could be.

Feed your intellect with logic, facts, models, and theories. Delight your senses and stimulate your creativity with stories, philosophy, and the most enchanting poetry. And awaken your spirit with a genuine call from the heart to treasure this gift of life with which we have all been blessed.

Paul offers us the opportunity to take a fresh look at our lives and our world and gives us tools to help make it a more positive one, both for ourselves and for those around us.

This is a manual for living. Read it to help you live, love, and learn. Absorb it to help you realize who you are meant to be and become - *The Super You.* And share *In Search of a Positive World* with others to help them do the same.

Enjoy the journey!

Lynn McLeod
Queste, Leadership Coaching and Training

Dedicated to all those I love

I am a lucky person to have such a wonderful family and friends

To my Wife, love is everything.

Also

Dedicated to the memories of the 96

You will never walk alone

'All you need is love'

- The Beatles

Contents

Introduction   *v*

The Search   *viii*

Prologue   *ix*

Chapter 1: The Sword in the Stone   1

Chapter 2: The Search (Footprints in the Sands of Time)   12

Chapter 3: The Inner Quest: A Sense of Purpose   23

Interlude 1: The Inner Guide   40

Chapter 4: The Soul & The Spirit   44

Chapter 5: The Will to Love   67

Chapter 6: The Super You   92

Interlude 2: Tale in the Making   119

Chapter 7: A Code for Life   130

Chapter 8: The Character   154

Chapter 9: A Way of Life   171

Interlude 3: The Search Continues   200

Chapter 10: Personal Mastery   207

Chapter 11: Characterisation - The Process of Becoming   223

Chapter 12: Special Attention   236

Interlude 4: The Messiah   252

Chapter 13: A Sense of Being: The Essence and The Realm   258

Interlude 5: The Magician   265

Epilogue: Evermore   267
Bibliography   274
Useful Websites   277
Special Thanks   278
Readers Feedback   279

The Search

Looking, hiding, running, what for?
What do we want? What can we have?
We search for that part which is missing,
Wishing, wanting, dreaming,
Wondering through ageless stars,
Searching through desert plains,
Climbing the highest mountains,
Thinking, walking, talking to find out
That we don't understand, that it is too much,
That the pain is great and the torment,
Feeling, crying, praying for fate to change,
Life is so realistically
Smashing and twisting our imagination
And sweet fantasies, our lost dreams,
Praying, taking, giving for nothing
Or is it something?
To make the most of life,
While we are alive,
While we breathe,
Searching, watching, falling through time
For life is short,
We age quickly,
Then comes the end.
Evaluation? Was it good? Was it bad?
Were we part of the great cycle?
Or did you and I diminish?
Was this life a shattered wasteland?
Or a tale in the making?
Was it your own personal hell?
Or Paradise on earth my sweet angel?
Who knows but still searching......
A question for you: Have you been searching?

Prologue

> 'Whatever you can do. Or dream you can. Begin it. Boldness has genius, power and magic in it. Begin it now.' - Goethe

---

Can I ask you a question? How are you feeling right now? Are you sitting comfortably? Are you relaxed in your environment? What feelings do you have in anticipation of this book? Excitement? A peppered interest? A vagueness? Or perhaps you are thinking 'let's just see how the first ten pages or so go – if it doesn't feel right then I don't have to browse any further'. Well let's start by getting the environment right for you to read this book – because I want to connect with your subconscious greater self and to do that I need you to be relaxed. So this is what we need to agree, that you will where possible create the right environment to lucidly read this book; whether you are fully relaxed by dimming the lights, allowing soft sweet music to play in the background or even to have a drink or two, so that you are now feeling deep in relaxation and therefore ready for illumination and a journey of exploration.

The next question then must be: What have you heard about Being and Becoming? What talk has there been, if any? In Search of a Positive World, does that sound right to you? Is that why you have chosen to read this book? Let's face it no one has ever bought or borrowed a book, which has been referred to as dull or monotonously boring. So open your ears and be prepared to become one with the musical orchestra playing in the background of this, your life's masterpiece.

Then what do you expect to see? Will the sun set with each word while the sea draws close to arrival? Will you be so dazzled by the content that you will be dancing by moonlight in the mirror of completeness? Will you perhaps see models and diagrams that can enrich and enlighten your soul? Well the curtain is ready to be drawn so on with the show of enlightenment and sweet ecstasy.

Are you looking to become all you can be? Do you want your life to be a tale in the making? Do you want the self-actualization to discover your great inner soul and spirit? Then read on denizen of the world....your time has come and your time is now - be prepared to analyse your own soul!

The Presenter (or is it the Magician to me?) And the Dialogue

He was a bold man; some said he was stretched when young because his potential seemed to flow from an endless sea. He was dark and mysterious in complexion with a jester's mischievous smile. He had prepared his presentation for the conference and he was ready to stand and deliver.

His mental preparation was that he was in a place of seemingly breathless state, at one with himself, at peace with the world. And so his chorus began.

After his energetic and lively introduction, he assessed how the audience was feeling, teasing them with what they would hear and by creating a visual expectation. He then exploded into tale.

"There were 2 boys, twins. They grew up playing together, but with a big difference. Seeing such a big disconcerting difference their mother grew worried for the boys. You see one little boy seemed to be positive and optimistic; in fact he was a daring, outgoing child. On the other hand, the other little boy was so very negative and pessimistic and was never truly willing to get involved or even have a go. This really worried the mother. So much so she decided to take them to see a doctor. The doctor checked them over and immediately noticed that the positive and optimistic boy was in extremely good health and the negative and pessimistic boy had been continuously ill. '*This is a strange case,*' he said to the mother. '*A case like this needs further analysis and exploration.*' The mother agreed to an experiment.

The doctor took the negative and pessimistic little boy and locked him in a room full of toys, sweets, chocolate, everything a little boy could possibly dream of. And then he left him there for hours to play.

He then took the optimistic and positive little boy and locked him in a room with a 12ft pile of horse manure, much to his mother's disapproval. And then he left him there to play.

A few hours later, they returned to the negative and pessimistic little boy, who had not moved from his chair.

'Well little boy, how come you have not moved?' he said in his deep South Carolina American accent, which was unusual in Liverpool.

'I didn't want to hurt myself sir.'

'What about the rocking horse boy?'

'I might have fallen off!'

'What about the football?'

'I might have kicked it and broken my ankle.'

'What about the sweets and lovely lollipops?' The doctor now sounded like the child-catcher from Chitty Chitty Bang Bang – which is enough to scare anyone!

'I didn't want to eat them in case I was sick.'

'God!' cried the doctor. 'This boy is seriously negative and pessimistic!'

They then left to go and see the other boy and upon opening the door they found horse manure everywhere - on the walls, on the ceiling, and all over the place.

The doctor, shocked, exclaimed: 'What on earth where you thinking laddie?' in his now American with a Scottish twang accent.

The boy replied: 'Well sir, with a pile of horse manure that big there had to be a pony in here somewhere!'

The crowd laughed.

"What does that tale tell you? Well let me tell you another story or two.

I heard a story the other day about a man who lost his family. It seems that in setting out on life's adventure he took the wrong turn. Where did that man go who worshipped his family? You see he decided that work was far more important and he spent more and more time at the office. He became distracted by his sport and socialized far too much with his friends…and then came the affairs - the spiral continued and you can guess what happened.….

Which reminds me of the man who just kept on winning – everywhere he went things fell into place. I met this man on what seemed (to be) like a train going nowhere which he convinced me was going everywhere. He told me of his life and how the world conspired to do him good. His glass was neither half empty nor half full but full to the top with abundance in good fortune. So I asked him how this was possible."

The audience awaited an answer as he left them hanging by changing the subject again.

"Did you know I have a special offer today? I will give anyone from the audience a ten pound note if they would be kind enough to let me borrow their shoes for the next ten minutes."

The audience laughed as he held up the shiny ten-pound note.

"I'll do it," said a man from the front row, obviously after a bit of attention. So they swapped the note for the shoes.

"So who will give me their socks for twenty pounds?" More laughter from the crowd. Next thing a young lady hands over her socks.

"I hope they're not yesterday's." "Oh no," she cried in dismay. The audience laughed again.

"Let's raise the stakes, who will give me their trousers for a £50 pound note?" Almost immediately two gentlemen started to strip.

"Ok, the one who gets their pants to me the fastest wins the £50 note." This became a race as the two men tried to strip as quickly as possible and race over to the presenter. At this point the audience was in stitches.

"You're a rather forthcoming lot – what about a blouse or shirt for £100 pounds. The next thing a lady gave up her blouse and sat there in her bra.

This was met with great approval by most men in the audience.

"So then, what is the point of the exercise?"

"We all have a price we are willing to pay."

"Money buys consumer goods."

"There is a limit to what money can buy." Suggestions sprang from the crowd.

"Really?" he said. "If I offered you a million pounds to strip naked who would do it?" Laughter again. "No seriously, who would do it? Let's have a show of hands."

Slowly and surely the whole audience raised their hands.

"Hmmm, interesting. So for a few million we could have a nudist colony at this conference." More laughter.

"So what is the point?" he asked.

"We can all be bought."

"Hmmm, interesting again – because the point to me in this story is not what money can buy but what the money represents…what does the money represent?"

"Capital."

"To do what?"

"To live the lifestyle you choose"

"Right, here is how I see it. I view the money (holding up lots of it in his hands) as your potential and existing ability to motivate and inspire yourself and other people. The money is the 'how', and you hold the money (which is your potential). It is 'who' you are and 'what' you decide to do with it that makes the difference!"

"If you choose to be a miser in life, what return will you get?" Silence.

"But if you choose to realize and give the money (your potential) and share the wealth, you can be rich beyond your wildest dreams."

"In giving of the money (your potential) you give positive energy through a purposeful special attention that will create not only a world full of direction but lifestyle opportunities for us all."

Silence from the audience.

"So let me ask you - why are you here today?"

"I remember sitting on that train when that man asked me the same question – *why are you here?* I replied nonchalantly: I am on my way home. Again he asked me - *why are you here?* Because I am. *No,* he said, *why are you here?* There was a silence. So I asked him why the world had been so kind to him – was it luck? *No,* he replied. *I live by my values and I prioritise my life to live in line with my values. I truly believe that the world is conspiring to do me good and through that I keep on winning. We all want to be winners and we all want to be associated with them,* he said. *But more importantly I give back more than what I take but for some reason I always get more in return. So why are you here?*

Now that reminds me of the guy who lost his family – why did that happen? Were his priorities wrong? His values? At what point did he lose his family? When he lost himself? When he continued to take from a half empty glass?

So Why Are You Here?

To finish with a quote from the famous German playwright Wolfgang Goethe:

"One can be master and win
Or serve and lose
Grieve or triumph
Be the anvil or the hammer."

The scene ends with a standing ovation and so with an end our journey begins.

Chapter 1:
The Sword in the Stone

"Still round the corner there may wait
A new road or a secret gate,
And though we may pass them by today,
Tomorrow we may come this way
And take the hidden paths that run
Towards the Moon or to the Sun."
- JRR Tolkien – The Lord of the Rings

Where is the starting point? Well the starting point is about making the decision to act and then continue to act. Most people in life only ever think about it, they think, 'Well I could have done this or I could have done that' and then life passes them by. They focus so much on the past or on the future that they forget the present: 'If only I had done that six months ago I could be thin for my holiday now'; 'I'll definitely start writing my book, start my business, decorate the house next week, next month, next year…..'.

Question: Where does our life exist?

Answer: In the present, never forsake it for the past or the future.

There is no such thing as the past or future, only present memories and changing present state.

So I have started and you are here reading along. I once sat in a class and we were asked to write down a goal that we would like to achieve in a new present state (The Future) and I wrote *'TO CHANGE THE WORLD'*. We then had to pass that goal around to the person on our left and when I passed mine over that person laughed and said *'You can't change the world'*.

How did that person's statement make me feel? Comments like that can promote negative energy. How you choose to react to comments, people, and life in general, is pivotal to your success in life. Well it made me feel even more determined to write this book, because I believe that anything is possible, that we can achieve almost anything we put our minds to and that we all have a multitude of undiscovered potential.

So why could I not change the world? And why can't I change the world in my own special way? Changing the world for me is writing this book to influence your life, and mine, for the better, hence changing aspects of the world or changing our world. I firmly believe that the world is evolving to become a better place and that we can find harmony in this day and age of war, famine, and over population. Surely what we want is to make this world a better place for our children instead of grabbing everything we can before we kick the bucket? We can do this by taking this life to the next spiritual level of existence and evolution, making this world a positive place to live.

In my world I live by three basic premises:

> *That there is something as opposed to nothing, so we should make the most of the something we have.*

In the world that I live in, there is something that exists as opposed to nothing. In fact, nothing itself cannot exist. If it were to exist, there would be nothing instead of something, and we all know that something exists. (Even if the something we know is through our senses.)

If that something exists then, in the truest form of respect, I appreciate every little bit of something around me and hence I believe we should make the most of that something, which is life and the world we live in.

> *Life is a continual cycle of being and becoming from birth to death.*

Life from birth is a continual cycle of being and becoming. When born we are simply being that evolves to become. In becoming, we realize our true sense of being which then enables us to stretch ourselves to become once more. In the Eastern world it is the sense of being that is found at the expense of becoming. In the Western world people strive so much to become that they find little contentment without a sense of being.

We are here to become all we can be.

Quite simply we are placed upon this planet, given the gift of this life, to become all we can be.

Now if we can agree with the above, or at least entertain me a little longer with those premises, then we have a starting point to act upon.

Question: Why read this book and listen to me?

Hmm, good question. **Answer:** To make us really think about our life; what you want out of life; to help you realize that your dreams are possible; that you can become all that you can be; that you can discover the **Super You**; that you are part of the pattern and that we can do this together.

And for me, it gives me the opportunity to challenge your way of thinking by sharing my philosophy in life so that we can achieve the above through raising our psychological intelligence; by re-programming our mind, to change the subterranean landscape of our subconscious and conscious mind; to live by new paradigms (ways of thinking); to develop a winning mindset that gives us the foundation to realize our full potential. For example:

I could believe I was born with an incredible mindset because I was born lucky – I was born on Friday 7th (a lucky day and number), in a lucky month (I am a Leo – such an outgoing sign), born in 1970 (a nice lucky round number with 7 in the year). I grew up with two sets of parents, my birth parents and a couple next door who could have no children and treated me as their own. I received all the love, and more, to make me a well-grounded and secure individual. I was born by Liverpool, a fun loving and lucky place where the people have such a wonderful sense of humour, which is unsurpassed! Jung called Liverpool the 'pool of life'.

I believe, and have always believed, that I was destined to do great things and that I am special and so are you.

Ok let's stop there, am I lucky? Perhaps to some people and to others maybe not, it depends if you believe in luck. I believe that we make our own luck through the choices and actions we take. I also believe there is a pattern we cannot escape but that we can shape.

In life the choices we make will shape our life and the mindset we have will determine our future or present new states.

And I also believe that life shapes and conditions us in so many ways that our destiny is part of the pattern.

A Date with Destiny

In 1989 I was astounded by what I can only call an incredible fate. It was a fate that I had surely felt nothing like before and have felt nothing like it since. On the 15th April we awoke after a night out in Sheffield and it was Semi-Final day in the FA Cup at Hillsborough. We had been the year before when we played and beat Nottingham Forest, and I had sat in the stand behind the goal in Leppings Lane.

This year we had tickets for the Leppings Lane terrace.

I remember taking a brisk walk that morning in the local park thinking how fresh and good life can be. After a few drinks we headed for the match and all I could think about was my awful hangover from the night before. When we got to the ground it was a similar sight to most big matches with large crowds outside the ground, a lack of police and a bit of pushing and shoving to get in the ground.

Tragically, Hillsborough turned into one of football's worst disasters. I remember getting there around 2:40pm, my friend and I getting nowhere as the crowd moved back and forwards outside the ground.

'We're on the march with Kenny's army, *we are* all going to Wembley and we'll really shake you up when we win the FA Cup cause Liverpool are the greatest football team.' Everyone was happy and singing.

I could remember seeing only one policeman on a horse and we dived under the horse to get in the ground within seconds. We darted down what was to become the tunnel of death and could barely see the pitch at three minutes to three. We tried to push in, but to no avail; my hangover was awful, I felt sick. So I suggested to my friend that we go round the other side - the only way you would ever have known there was another side was if you had been there the year before. At two minutes to three, the gate collapsed, letting in hundreds of Liverpool fans who ran down that tunnel of death. The rest is history. We watched from the terrace as fans were being crushed to death at the fencing at the front by the pitch. And more people died in that tunnel. We had escaped by less than a minute.

I remember being lifted up in the stands and watching the horror from above. We watched as a fan was carried to the side of the pitch and they started to give him the kiss of life. I felt cold....

Eventually the pitch was overtaken by bodies; men, women, girls and children were screaming, crying, as we watched with disbelief and in shock. (My cousin who was a Doctor told us later he went on to the pitch to help the victims and a Father was begging him not to leave his young daughter...she was dead...he had to move on to another victim... another of my cousins was helping out by using the advertising boards as stretchers to help get victims to the ambulances.)

We watched in the stands, paralyzed. There is only so long you can watch people dying before something starts to die inside of you.

I remember walking out the stands and there was a guy the size of a giant, motionless on the floor. He had been lifted up out of the crowd. We walked out dazed and still in shock. I just wanted to see my Father.

And how relieved my Father was when we met him after the game - he had been waiting for me up the road - in fact he was possibly the first person to leave the game. Upon leaving he asked a policeman to open the gate to let him out. The policeman had said the game could not have been that bad, if it had even started. My Father told him that people were dying in there, much to the policeman's disbelief. How happy he was on my return and how lucky we were to be alive, and to be breathing.

It was unclear what was going on. As we now know, 96 fans died that day – the day *'we were'* all going to Wembley. You will never ever really truly understand a disaster unless you are there; you can empathize but you will never understand.

For two weeks afterwards, I walked around in a haze, guilty that I was alive, and for years the sound of an ambulance would haunt me.

But this book is not about Hillsborough; it's about what Hillsborough taught me. And that is - we are all special; no one deserves to die and there is a pattern in life that we can shape but that we can't escape. It taught me that life is a gift and we should make the most of every day and attempt to become all that we can be.

It also taught me that, in times of great need, such as a disaster, people can work together no matter what colour or creed; that they share grief and loss as if it were their own through a heavenly compassion.

I was lucky to be alive; we all are.

Belief: I am lucky to be alive and every day is a blessing.

To the other extreme, one of the most wonderful experiences in my life was the birth of my beautiful daughter, India Jade. The birth experience has to be one of the most exhilarating moments in life that lifts one to another plain of existence.

The miracle of life is that life finds a way.

Belief: Life is a gift.

Now let's explore a number of scenarios that will help us to explore our inner self and identify our true motivation in life. Complete the exercises as you go along.

The Sword and the Stone

King Luther was defeated in battle even though he wielded the mighty blade Excalibur. In trying to escape his foe within nearby woods he was set upon by dark knights and mortally wounded, so he cast Excalibur into a massive lump of stone, forcing the sword so deep that only the hilt could be seen. King Luther swore that only his rightful bloodline would be able to lift the sword before being slain. Merlin feared for King Luther's son, Arthur, and took him into hiding. For years the land was Kingless, for no one could pull the sword from the stone. Only brave knights who proved themselves in feats of valour, such as jousting, were allowed to attempt to lift the sword from the stone. The bravest and most daring knights all came in vain to lift the sword and take their place as King.

If you were a Knight who won the jousting competition, what would you do about the sword?

What would you be thinking before lifting the sword?

If you failed to free the sword, what would you be thinking afterwards?

If you were a peasant who was not allowed to attempt to draw the sword, what would you be thinking?

What if you were a boy in the woods?

And upon pulling the sword you became King, what would you then think?

Let's review the situations. If you were a brave knight who had the opportunity to draw Excalibur, what would you do? Well I am sure you would take the opportunity to draw the sword because that is the reason you were there. What would be going through your mind? That it could be you? Sounds a bit like the modern lottery! Or perhaps you would be thinking no one has done it before so it would not be possible. Then upon the sword not moving, what would be your belief, knowing you are one of the strongest knights in the land? That it would take a giant to lift the sword? Or would you go back to everyone and tell them that because you couldn't do it, nobody else should even try? It's just not possible. It would take a miracle, I mean if you couldn't do it, how should anyone else expect to? Would you perhaps think you were a failure because you failed and then let that affect the rest of your life? *I'm just not good enough…what could have been….if only….*

If you were a peasant how would you feel and think? You're not even allowed to try to lift the sword. Would you settle for a life of mediocrity because you are not of Royal blood? Or would you dare to dream?

And lastly, what of the boy? What would you be thinking as a boy? What would you be dreaming? *'I am the bravest White Knight of the West who defeats the Black Knight to become King of all the lands.'* So would the boy think twice about drawing the sword when no one is looking? Of course he wouldn't, especially if he were like the optimistic twin from the story at the conference earlier.

And then, when he does lift the sword, the nearest peasant tells him to place it back even though it hasn't been done before - talk about conditioning.

However, a nearby knight catches wind of this and comes to draw the sword himself and when he tries he is unsuccessful even though the sword has been placed back by the boy. So he demands that the boy draw the sword and, in front of many knights and people, the boy Arthur draws the sword. The impossible dream is made possible.

The knight who had just failed, being wise, then kneels to his King, kissing the blade Excalibur. What would you be thinking then? 'Oh my God I am King?' 'Oh my God, a bit like winning the lottery with a lot more responsibility?' Would you be scared, afraid, anxious, happy, or overwhelmed? You are now to be stretched beyond belief, a boy to a king. But does the boy take it in his stride? How doubtful and stressed would you as an adult be if I were to name you King or Queen of England? Hmm, a mixed response, but really think about what you would have to do and, yes, I bet you wouldn't have a problem with all that money! (But then we are all Kings and Queens in our own right.)

So what is the point? The simple point I am making from the story of Arthur and the sword in the stone is that we are all conditioned in life from birth. We are totally reactive to every experience we encounter and those experiences can completely shape our lives. Our parents, our upbringing, our schools, our town, our society, our culture, and the history of the world condition us. We develop mental models about every form of stimuli in life and form deeply ingrained assumptions, generalizations and images, which influence how we understand and respond.

> *We are born to win but conditioned to lose, just like in the scenario above.*

In that scenario, how were the different levels of people conditioned to think? The knight may have thought that it was not possible, and when he failed, that it would never be possible. The peasants are considered not even worthy or good enough, yet the young boy who has the mindset of a child thinks that anything is possible and so are his dreams.

Why then do so many people give up on their dreams as they grow up? Because a lot of the time they are conditioned to fail or conform to mediocrity either because it would take a lot of hard work or that they would have to stand out to be different. But in this day and age of opportunity, something is possible that allows modern man to pursue his dreams with the right mindset and motivation.

So why should we be motivated to live at all?

> *In the Kingdom of Heaven we are all angels, on earth we are vast potential awaiting discovery…so let's spread our wings and ride the sands of time together.*

Life Changing Questions

What are the premises you live your life by?
What do you think about life?
Why do you think we exist?
What are your dreams?
What are you willing to give to achieve your dreams?
How full is your glass in life?

What mental models are holding you back from realizing your
   potential?

How does your past affect the person you are?

How are you creating your own world?

How true are you being to yourself?

> *"My life has been full of terrible misfortunes, most of which never happened." - Michel De Montaigne*

> *The man opened his arms to embrace you with the world complete in his demeanor, then he spoke: 'Welcome to the real world – open your eyes deep within your very soul and see yourself for the first time, who are you?*
>
> *Where are you going? Why do you search? Why are you here?'*

Summary

1. That there is something as opposed to nothing, so we should make the most of the something we have.

2. Life is a continual cycle of being and becoming from birth to death.

3. We are here to become all that we can be.

4. We shape our life and our life shapes us.

5. Life is a gift.

6. We are born to win but conditioned to lose.

7. We tend to give up on our childhood dreams.

8. With the right mindset and motivation, the achievement of our dreams is possible.

> *"Every man, wherever he goes, is encompassed by a cloud of comforting convictions, which move with him like flies on a summer's day." - Bertrand Russell*

Chapter 2: The Search (Footprints in the Sands of Time)

"He who has a why to live for can bear almost any how."
- Friedrich Nietzsche

What motivates man to live? Why should man choose to live at all, considering all the suffering, pain and death in this world that offers little comfort in remorse and little understanding of why we exist at all? Why does man strive to explore, to build, to create, when he fully understands the mortality of his own fate? Why should man believe in more than one life in the form of consolation for the truth that perhaps in the end it ends?

What motivates man to live?

Travelling back through time there are two conflicting theories of where we came from, that of evolution and that of God. (There could be a third dependent upon your beliefs that perhaps we were placed on this planet by aliens.) Taking evolution first – the concept explains we have evolved from apes and our natural instinct is to survive and procreate, hence survival of the fittest. There is some hard evidence through skull examination of Neanderthal Man for example, however, I have never got past the point that if we evolved from apes why do apes still exist? Then there is the theory or religious belief that God created the world and all living things within it. If we travel back through time we can trace the stories of the bible and the characters within it, and have some conclusive proof those figures really existed. It's interesting to think that dinosaurs roamed the earth for millions of years, yet we have less than ten thousand years recorded history. Our natural instinct, like any animal, is to survive yet we have transcended the animal kingdom to rule over the Earth – we have been motivated by our needs to survive in the past because the landscape dictated our priorities.

In prehistoric times we hunted to survive and naturally became very skilled and extremely fit. This changed with the knowledge of agriculture, and farming became an easier way to produce food to survive. Farming became the main form of survival for hundreds of years with markets and trade routes opening up across Europe. We then moved from farming to an industrial landscape where there became two clear classes within society - the factory owners/managers and the working class. There had been different classes previously, based on nobility and land ownership. From the Industrial Society we then moved towards a production based society, after the 2nd World War moving towards new industries through technology and a more certain time with unemployment low. With the advent of television and the media we have moved to a consumer based society with our motivation changing to wants as opposed to needs, to our desired chosen lifestyle with life opportunities opening to most people, although conditioning and conformity meant that most stayed in their stratified groups. Over the last 20 years we have seen the knowledge explosion through the easy access of all kinds of information through the Internet and the media. Altering working life so that office jobs, retail, and contact centres, which require the flexing of mental muscles as opposed to the physical nature of the production and industrial labour, have become the major sources of employment.

With so much information available we are now faced with the assessment of all possibilities – globalization has meant the world is easily accessible through travel and trading markets. New dangers exist through terrorism and detailed information is readily available on every risk we take, when eating, drinking, driving, and so on.

How simple must life have been in pre-historic times, when our motivation was to survive, provide for the tribe and to worship the sun? Now how diverse is the world with complexity through complete choice – old structures of living are broken down to offer every individual the choice to be who they want to be, to do what they want to do, to go where they want to go. Sounds like the Martini advert...your life in a nutshell you can be anytime, anywhere, any place...you can be anything you want to be.

A lot of people find that far too complicated because it requires them to take accountability for their own lives, their own outcomes.

And over the years, mankind's bedrock of a belief has been threatened, that we come from a good gracious God Almighty who created the world - n fact we could see him everyday because he was the sun. At some point we had several Gods to worship with myths differing from region to region with lots of similarities, e.g., the great flood can be found in the Bible and the Koran. Over the years our paradigm of the world has changed, firstly with Galileo because the world is in fact round, with Darwin and evolution, and more recently with the new world religion of science. A greater belief in science has meant a loss of religious and mythical beliefs that mankind's deep sense of being, his bedrock, his very foundation, has been lost with his footprints in the sands of time.

The world would now seem such a chaotic place to prehistoric man that our transition means we have moved from a state of naturalness to complexity and neurosis. We are challenged to rise above the subterranean passages of a life pre-ordained to make the choices to move beyond conformity and comfort.

So what motivates man to live in this day and age of reason?

I would like to explore one such answer, Viktor Frankl's, which was induced through suffering, a great suffering. Frankl is an internationally renowned psychiatrist who endured years in the Nazi concentration camps of complete horror. Frankl created his own form and approach to psychotherapy which he called logotherapy. At the core of his theory is the belief that man's primary motivational force is his search for meaning.

Frankl wrote about the 'will to meaning' being the primary motivation in life.

> "*Man's search for meaning is the primary motivation in his life and not a 'secondary rationalization' of instinctual drives. This meaning is unique and specific in that it must and can be fulfilled by him alone; only then does it achieve a significance which will satisfy his own will to meaning. There are some authors who contend that meanings and*

values are 'nothing but defense mechanisms, reaction formations and sublimations'. But as for myself, I would not be willing to live merely for the sake of my 'defense mechanisms', nor would I be ready to die merely for the sake of my 'reaction formations'. Man, however, is able to live and even die for the sake of his ideals and values!

A public-opinion poll was conducted a few years ago on France. The results showed that 89 percent of the people polled admitted that man needs 'something' for the sake of which to live. Moreover, 61 percent conceded that there was something or someone, in their lives for whose sake they were even ready to die. I repeated this poll at my Hospital department in Vienna among both the patients and the personnel, and the outcome was practically the same as among the thousands of people screened in France; the difference was only 2 percent.

Another statistical survey, of 7948 students at forty-eight colleges, was conducted by social scientists from John Hopkins University. Their preliminary report is part of a two year study sponsored by the National Institute of Mental Health. Asked what they considered "very important" to them now, 16 percent of the students checked "making a lot of money"; 78 percent said their first goal was finding a purpose and meaning to my life." - Viktor Frankl – In Search for Meaning

Frankl goes on to explain that man's will to meaning can also be frustrated in what he terms existential frustration. The frustration can be in existence or being itself, the meaning of existence or the striving to find a meaning and can result in neuroses. He explains: *"Existential frustration is in itself neither pathological nor pathogenic. A man's concern, even despair, over the worthlessness of life is an existential distress but by no means a mental disease."*

In this day and age of uncertainty and diversity what Frankl terms as existential frustration is that lack of meaning or purpose. It is the hopelessness in life where the individual is either yet to find a way or has ended up lost, shaped by life to become a reactive being in limbo. As we grow from the naturalness of childhood we are shaped by every experience - this conditioning of life programs deep in to the subconscious creating a subterranean landscape - our map of the world. In fact we move from a natural state to a complex state that can end up as deep neurosis or personality disorders. Dependent upon the stress of each experience and how we cope depends upon the complexes we form. For our growth it would seem essential to have a range of positive/good and negative/bad experiences to develop inner character.

Frankl suggests: *"I consider it a dangerous misconception of mental hygiene to assume that what man needs in the first place is equilibrium or, as it is called in biology, "homeostasis," i.e., a tensionless state. What man actually needs is not a tensionless state but rather the striving and struggling for a worthwhile goal, a freely chosen task. What he needs is not a homeostasis but what I call "noo-dynamics" i.e., the existential dynamics in a polar field of tension where one pole is represented by a meaning that is to be fulfilled and the other pole by a man who has to fulfill it."*

Frankl asserts that there is no holistic meaning to life but that it differs from man to man, day to day, hour from hour.

And that man should not ask what the meaning to life is but recognize that it is he who is asked.

One answers for one's own life.

According to Frankl, *"…we can discover this meaning in life in three different ways: 1. By creating a work or doing a deed; This is through creative values where the providing of meaning comes from one's creative projects or the project of one's life. Frankl views creativity as a function of the spiritual unconscious, which he calls conscience. 2. By experiencing something or encountering someone (The second way of finding a meaning in life is by experiencing something – such as goodness, truth and beauty – by experiencing nature and culture or, last but not least, by experiencing another human being in his very uniqueness – by loving him); and 3. by the attitude we take toward unavoidable suffering."*

What a revelation Frankl was for me. When growing up I was a true romantic born of a great heritage of traditional family values, truth, honesty, integrity, good manners, and an appreciation of the value of human relationship and the importance of love.

I was a born daydreamer who first discovered himself creatively by playing with toys in the most imaginative way, providing meaning for the child. Each game had a story, a meaning, a direction that represented eternity in life. Then I would develop the concept of the subjective 'I' in full by conjuring the belief that the whole world evolved around me. In fact there was no world without me so when I died the world died with me. Then artistically I would attempt to paint my feelings upon canvass, much to the dismay of my teachers. So what if I liked Dali and Freud at an early age and my paintings were surreal in taste with names such as 'The Madness of Tranquility'?

Then I discovered poetry in combination with the art, and continually felt the weight of history upon my young shoulders. Poems entitled 'The Search' and 'The Lonely World' only pointed towards my own indistinguishable search for meaning at an early age and the imaginations that I was responsible for discovering some ultimate truth in life. As teenagers or students we are searching for meaning in life because we are naïve and lacking in life experience, no matter character. It is such an existential shame that so many young people find life hopeless or meaningless and that so few then go into life to find that meaning. When younger we are plagued by the search for ultimate explanation because we are scared of the aloneness of life – unfortunately too many never pass this adolescent stage.

For me to find Frankl at such a late age, of 35, was such a revelation because I finally found a writer (psychiatrist) who had penned down on paper a lot of my inner beliefs when younger.

So there we have it – what motivates man to live?

Having a meaning to life - individual meaning – a meaning to be fulfilled!

What a great starting point for a book about motivation and personal development. Nothing you don't already know?

On the point of homeostasis, a tensionless state of being, I would like to introduce Schopenhauer who said: "So long as we are given to the throng of desires with its constant hopes and fears...we never obtain lasting happiness or peace." He also goes on to explain: "Motives and causes are experienced from within." Arthur Schopenhauer was born in Danzig in 1788. He was in his twenties when he wrote his masterpiece 'The World as Will & Representation' published in 1818.

Schopenhauer stressed that through our perception what we believe is my body is really my will. For the body is the appearance of which will is the reality. The essence of his theory, which relates to Immanuel Kant's separation of the phenomenal and noumenal worlds, is that there are two aspects of the self: the self as it appears phenomenally as an object of perception (objectively, as idea, as I experience all other objects in the world) and the self as it is in itself, noumenally, as a manifestation of will.

My will is to be identified with the will of the whole universe and as a result of my subjective perception my separateness is a complete illusion. Within nature it is universal will that is vast and real.

> *A way from within stands open to us to that real inner nature of things to which we cannot penetrate from without, it is so to speak, a subterranean passage, a secret alliance, which as if by treachery places us all at once in the fortress that could not be taken from outside.'*
> *- Schopenhauer.*

To find the subterranean passage Schopenhauer mentions, we have to realize that we ourselves are the thing in itself and we have to realize we are among the things we require to know. Our real essence is will and the subjective 'I', which we believe to be 'me', is only apparent to ourselves in the world of phenomena. The will is universal, it is a force which does not belong to the individual, rather it is entombed in the individual by its great desire to manifest itself in the world of appearances. It rages through individual being in an attempt to reveal itself in the outer world.

Schopenhauer believed the will should be resisted at all cost for we are at the mercy of the will and because it is the foundation of the universe it is the cause of all our suffering.

It shapes everything we do and we are bound like slaves to its demands. Its energy is like a poison infiltrating the way we think and act, leading to our suffering through desire and insatiable greed of will. Universal will is eternal being essential to all life and our suffering increases with raised awareness and increase of knowledge.

> 'There arises within him a horror of the nature of which his own phenomenal existence is an expression, the kernal and inner nature of that world which is recognised full of misery.' - Schopenhauer.

For human beings are not essentially rational but are desiring, emotional animals whose rationality was developed to serve and maximise the will to life. David Bergman narrates that 'Schopenhauer's pessimism explains the cause of our discontent, which lies in the substance of the world- in its being will to life. Life in short is: 1. Morally wrong. 2. Has no meaning or purpose. 3. Will always have more pain than pleasure. So there is ultimately nothing we can do to alter this worst of possible worlds – except to end it by strangling all desire, thereby achieving what the Buddhists call Nirvana, which is the state closest to pure nothingness.'

> 'We must banish the dark impression of that nothingness which we discern behind all virtue and holiness as their final goal, and which we fear as children fear the dark; we must not evade it like Indians through myths and meaningless words, such as reabsorbtion in Brahma or the Nirvana of the Buddhists. Rather do we freely acknowledge that what remains after the entire of will is for all those who are still full of will certainly nothing; but conversely, to those in whom the will has turned and has denied itself, this our world, which is so real, with all its suns and milky ways – is nothing.' - Schopenhauer

Here is the essence of duality: optimism and pessimism. With optimism we assume that the universe exists to please us; with pessimism that it exists to displease us. In Scopenhauer's view it is here to displease us, for Frankl we should find meaning to please us.

It is this apparent duality in life which at times throws us into disorganized chaos. Western culture is very goal orientated and the god or gods are outward figures or representations, whereas the Eastern world is very much a place of inner being where my godhead or form is found within through meditation. We find duality in life all around us and many times we are left to ponder which road to take. Many roads are full of contradiction or escape logical explanation. But it is through logical explanation that man has created a dualistic world.

Surely if any god were to exist he would transcend the concepts of good and evil, wrong and right; or does the supreme being wage war of cosmic proportions against the forces of evil?

Eastern culture would renounce all desires and classification so there is a singular meaning through being and nature and their inner realization.

Life offers choices of duality in paths of life.

> *"Thus, the transitoriness of our existence in no way makes it meaningless. But it does constitute our responsibleness; for everything hinges upon our realising the essential transitory possibilities. Man constantly makes his choice concerning the mass of present potentialities; which of these can be condemned into non-being and which will be actualized? Which choice will be made an actuality once and forever, an immortal, "footprint in the sands of time"? At any moment, man must decide, for better or for worse, what will be the monument of his existence." – Frankl*

We search for that part which is missing and it is through meaning that we potentially fill the void of not understanding why we are here. The search for forever is the search for that part of us that perhaps knows the answers to everything, yet man's free will lies in his forgetting of that part which is missing. We might not understand everything but what we can understand is that it is our choice; we are accountable for our life, we are in control and so we decide how we should live our life. We can choose our footprints in the sands of time in search of our soul in making the most of the something we have.

What do you choose?
Life Changing Questions

What motivates you to live?

What is your meaning to life?

What gives you meaning in life?

Where do you come from?

Where are you now?

Where are you going?

What is your concept of the world?

What do you choose for your world?

What type of world do you live in – one filled with optimism and meaning or pessimism and suffering?

> *"Expect the unexpected or you'll never find it." - Heraclitus*

> *Walking beside the magician you come upon a hilltop seeing many a people taking paths in opposite directions, some with a will to embrace life, others taken by its insatiable cosmic will and he cried:*
>
> *'Where do you choose to live- in the dark or in the light?"*

Summary

1. Frankl suggests the will to meaning as being the primary motivation in life.

2. He also suggests that one answers for one's own life.

3. Schopenhauer says that so long as we give in to our desires we can never obtain lasting happiness or peace.

4. Frankl's philosophy is about finding meaning in your life through either creating a work or doing a deed, by experiencing something or someone or by the attitude we take toward unavoidable suffering. In comparison, Schopenhauer suggested life is morally wrong, it has no meaning or purpose and that there will always be more pain than pleasure. Frankl's view is one of partaking in life whilst Schopenhauer's is one of observing life in contrast the opposites of being and becoming in life.

5. You need to decide what your concept of the world is.

6. We search to understand life but it is in the not understanding that we are truly free. It at times seems that we once knew and that we have chosen to forget.

7. It's your choice - you are in control and are fully accountable for your own life, you choose your own premises for life built around your concept of the world, your own subterranean map of the world, determining your own internal state.

8. Challenge your pre-conditioned landscape of the mind and create a world full of meaning and joy.

   "The significant problems we face cannot be solved at the same level of thinking we were at when we created them." - Albert Einstein

Chapter 3: The Inner Quest: A Sense of Purpose

"We will either find a way or make one." – Hannibal

So we can choose our own concept of the world. We can also choose our own premises as to what we base our life upon and we can choose our own meaning to life - that's a lot of accountability, wouldn't you say? In moving forwards then to explore what motivates us to live, and from a very logical left brained approach, let's look at what motivation is and the different theories of motivation.

What is motivation? Quoting the dictionary definition:

Motivate; cause to act in a particular way, stimulate the interest.

Motive; the factor that induces a person to act, concerns with movement.

Let's simply focus on the key words in these descriptions and definitions.

Cause	Act
Stimulate	Interest
Factor	Induces
Concerned	Movement

So when we are motivated, are we carrying out an interesting moving action that is stimulated or induced by cause or factors? Therefore to be self-motivated there has to be an underlying reason for motivating ourselves to do the things we do. The word 'motivation' is derived from the Latin verb "movere" which means 'to move'. Motivation can therefore be described as 'something that moves you to action'. This something we will determine as the reason why a person acts in a certain way; therefore to understand motivation we need an understanding of the reasons why we want to achieve goals and also to prioritize them in an order that makes attainment of the goal through direct effort achievable.

> *'Motivation is an internal state that, when activated, changes behaviour through a desire, need or want.'*

Motivation can be linked to pain and pleasure in the sense that we may be considerably motivated to achieve certain pleasure or avoid certain pain, which would provide the reason for the consistent change in behaviour. When the desire for pleasure or the need to move away from pain is great so too is the motivation to change; when the desire or need is low in comparison then the motivation to achieve the goal will obviously decrease.

Identifying exactly what the pleasurable goal is or the avoidable pain or consequence of continuing action will enlighten us as to the reasons we are motivated. By using the picture of the end result it will enable us to motivate ourselves to achieve consistently. This visual picture helps to generate the feelings to maintain the motivation.

Generally most people are reactive in life; they wait for things to happen to them before making a commitment to change or to be consistently motivated to achieve the goal. Being reactive for example means that we wait to put weight on before we act, e.g., diet, exercise, which means that we are driven by pain or dissatisfaction to motivate us. Reactive motivation means that we tend to live by the pain principle. The proactive approach seeks pleasure. This is where we evaluate our life and through a desire, need or want we will be motivated consistently to achieve the pleasure it will provide.

This also relates to the stick and the carrot theory. For example, some people are motivated by criticism (pain), while others are motivated by praise and recognition (pleasure). In work what do people generally prefer - criticism or praise? In most cases it will be praise; however, in our own life, it tends to be our criticism of ourselves that motivates us.

So why is it in our personal life that we are driven reactively by the pain or dissatisfaction principle – where our own self-talk is critical before we act?

This will be explored further by taking a look at man's ultimate driving force and by seeking the ultimate explanation for motivation in later chapters.

In general, motivation can be separated into two categories: extrinsic (outside the person) or intrinsic (inside the person). Extrinsic motivation means the individual is motivated by external factors such as tangible rewards, salary, benefits, security, promotion, work environment, incentives. Intrinsic motivation means to be motivated by internal factors such as psychological rewards, opportunity, challenge, recognition, praise, sense of achievement, and so on.

For example, a person who is extrinsically motivated would need others to confirm how good they were at a given skill and they would need a lot of it. The intrinsically motivated person would find confirmation from inside themselves; they would still like to be told but will not seek that confirmation. In fact the extrinsically motivated person would revel in external praise where the intrinsically motivated person might be embarrassed by it.

What are you extrinsically motivated by?

What are you intrinsically motivated by?

Our focus should be what exactly motivates an individual to achieve or continually take action with persistence as opposed to being motivated to achieve the smaller things occasionally.

There is an endless list of possible reasons for being motivated that link to the pain and pleasure principle. It may be *Behavioural* to obtain a desired reward or escape unpleasant consequences; it could be *Physiological* through the senses, arousal, hunger, thirst etc; it could be *Social* in wanting to be part of a group or be like another; *Cognitive* in solving problems, making decisions, developing meaning or understanding; *Emotional* to increase feeling good or bad or to maintain feeling good about the self or *Self-Esteem* through status, achievement or recognition; *Conative* to take control of your life or obtain an individual dream; or perhaps *Spiritual* in attempting to understand why we are here.

'To persistently be motivated you need to feel with a burning desire or passion about a thing to continue to take action.'

Let's focus on theories of motivation starting with humanistic theories.

Maslow's Hierarchy of Needs

Abraham Maslow was born in 1908 in New York. He developed his humanistic theory, the Hierarchy of Needs model, in the 1940s -50s. His key work was the book 'Motivation & Personality', published in 1954. Maslow's theory was delivered through his research with monkeys. He established that, by withholding certain things, monkeys would develop a hierarchy of needs, i.e. when starved and without water then the monkeys would appropriately quench their thirst before devouring food henceshowing the thirst to be the greater need, and so on.

Maslow's Hierarchy of Needs is a five-stage model, and is built on the idea that man is motivated by his needs. We satisfy these needs in turn starting with the basic need for survival and then working through each following need. The needs form levels within a hierarchical triangle and only when the lower needs are met do we aspire to the next level.

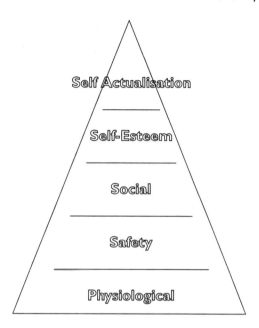

For example, once the physiological and safety needs have been met then we would move towards the belonging needs as our prime motivation, but if the safety needs suddenly become threatened, e.g., you are with friends (Belonging Needs) on a night out and someone attacks you then your motivation would be fight or flight (Safety Needs). This would also be the same if you were out with a group of people and you became hungry, then you would automatically seek food and forget about the group needs until the hunger need had been satisfied.

1. Physiological Needs, e.g., air, drink, shelter, warmth, sleep, avoiding pain, having sex.

2. Safety Needs, e.g., protection from the elements of the environment, order, stability, promotion, safe circumstances.

3. Love & Belonging Needs, e.g., the need for friends, family, love, affection, relationships, sense of community, work groups, being part of something.

4. Esteem Needs, e.g., respect from others, status, achievement, independence, recognition, glory, attention, reputation, confidence, dominance, prestige.

5. Self-Actualisation. These needs are becoming all you can be, realizing your full potential, self-fulfillment, value-driven, appreciation of life. Mankind's highest form of need is self-actualization.

Maslow's theory was developed further years later whereupon adapted versions of the model included for example in the first instance after esteem needs, cognitive needs (knowledge & meaning), aesthetic needs (appreciation of beauty), then self actualization needs and then transcendence needs (helping others achieve self actualization).

Maslow's model led to additional attempts to designing a holistic model of motivation. Leonard, Beavous and Scholl (1995) proposed five key sources of motivation:

1. Instrumental Motivation (Reward & Punishment)

2. Intrinsic Process Motivation (Enjoyment & Fun)

3. Goal-Internalisation (Set Values & Goals)

4. Internal Self-Concept Based (Behaviour matched to internal ideal self)

5. External Self-Concept Based (Behaviour matched to external ideal self)

Maslow gives us an appreciation of mankind's drivers and needs and how they need to be satisfied before moving to the next, as do Leonard, Beavous and Scholl who describe different sources of motivation.

Understanding the needs, sources and drivers preludes the search for the ultimate motivation, the ultimate force that drives us and which can be used to positively reinforce behaviour to achieve the vast sea of possibilities.

There are other content theories such as those of Alderfer and Herzberg, which relate to work. Alderfer's model condenses Maslow's into three levels of needs based on Existence needs such as sustaining existence and survival, and physiological and safety needs. Relatedness needs such as relationships, being part of a group, love, belonging, meaningful relationships. Growth needs such as self esteem, self-actualization, improving potential. The difference with Alderfer's theory is that the hierarchy is not the driver, all needs may be activated at the same time and frustration in one could lead to advanced pursuit of another even if it is the lower need.

Herzberg's Motivation-Hygiene model or theory states there are two sets of factors present. One set is comprised of dissatisfiers or 'hygiene factors' concerned with job environment and extrinsic to the job. These factors prevent dissatisfaction. The other set of factors are the motivators. These lead to growth, and are not linked to dissatisfaction, purely the feelings of satisfaction being achieved or not. This can be broken down into dissatisfactional motivators (Maintenance) such as money, job security, work environment, etc and then satisfiers (Growth) such as recognition, responsibility, interesting work, a sense of achievement.

Herzberg's theory ties in with the pain and pleasure principle in the sense that most people are driven or motivated by disatissfaction in life more so than the satisfiers or growth motivators. To most individuals, in life in general, it takes a lot of dissatisfaction before a real concerted effort is made to attain a goal on a consistent basis. For example, when an individual is pushed too far by the boss, they may eventually seek new employment, when possibly it was the individual holding himself or herself back - whether they actually leave is another matter. Again this links to associations to pain and pleasure. When dissatisfied enough with pain we become motivated to act but we are being totally reactive to the situation. When driven by pleasure or growth needs it is proactive measures or steps that help us to achieve through the needs desire.

Taking proactive measures in life will result in a consistent motivation which is driven by individual meaning, aspiration and achievement.

Cognitive theories of motivation – there are several other theories, which are processing theories of motivation. Leon Festinger's theory of Cognitive Dissonance suggests that when there is a discrepancy between two beliefs or actions we will act to resolve the conflict and discrepancy. The essence is that if we think positively about a belief but deep down in our subconscious we feel quite negative about that belief then there is a disagreement that needs to be resolved. Generally the one we believe the most will be the chosen belief or association and hence drive behaviour. However if we create enough disequilibrium then we can change the patterns of our behaviour and hence change our habits.

Generally the theory of Cognitive Dissonance suggests we seek 'Homeostasis' in our lives, remaining within our comfort zones, giving balance to our lives and therefore resisting change.

Another cognitive theory is Vroom's Expectancy Theory, which relies on three factors illustrated below.

Motivation = Expectancy x Instrumentality x Valance

Expectancy = Perceived probability of achievement or success

Instrumentality = Success & Reward

Valance = Value of obtaining the goal

All three must be high in order for motivation and positive change in behaviour to be high and they are very closely linked to Intrinsic and Extrinsic goals.

Other theories of motivation tend to be psychoanalytical or spiritual theories. Frankl asserts that man's ultimate motivation is the search for meaning, Jung the search for the soul or personal meaning. Freud's ultimate drivers were life (sexual) and death (aggressive) based around the will to pleasure, Adler asserts the will to power.

It is the spiritual line of thought that I would like to explore further. Before we take that course, let's focus on what makes us act in a certain way. To identify what makes us act in a certain way we need to establish the 'what's' in our life.

It's winter at half five in the morning. It's freezing outside and it's two hours before you have to get up to get ready to go to work. You have promised yourself you will get up to go jogging because you need to maintain your health, improve fitness and lose weight - very good reasons to rise at such an early hour of the day. It's 5.30am and the alarm goes off. What do you do? Get up to go running or take the extra couple of hours sleeping and tell yourself you will do it tomorrow, or the next day? What is it that motivates someone to get up at 5.30am everyday to go running 10 miles or play golf in summer before work? Surely this something that drives you to do such a thing has to be the greatest need, love, emotion or feelings to be so dedicated and committed to achieve such a high level of discipline and self-mastery?

So what is it that makes us act in a certain way, is it a free will that is a will to power or a will to love or a will to act? To be motivated or self motivated we have to decide to do something. Our level of commitment is derived from our self-discipline, attitude and how we condition ourselves to act to achieve goals. It's a simple fact we can't get motivated unless we have a reason that is empowered by emotion or feeling. So we need to find something in our life that provides a passion that will motivate. In a sense it is a meaning to be motivated by. So we need to establish the 'what's' in our life.

Once we have established the 'what's' which give you clear direction then, as Hannibal said, 'we will either find a way or make one'.

You need to have an innate sense of purpose and a goal.

It is this internal locus that will motivate an individual long term to achieve the lifestyle they want to live. For example we are not motivated by money but the things money can provide.

What is your internal motivation? What is driving you?

31

Now make a list of the 'what's' – what you want out of life.

This understanding of the 'what' we want in life gives us an internal singular motivation that can be described by listening to our feelings and thoughts about what we really desire and what we want to achieve from life - that inner purpose and goal.

Now we have established what we want out of life it is now important to consider what we are willing to pay. Making any additions to the list above link all the pain or dissatisfaction you will go through if you don't get what you want and next to that link all the pleasure you will get if you get or achieve what you want. Take time to work through each one and then consider how it makes you feel.

PAIN	PLEASURE

You have now established objectives and reasons so now you need to take action, which is cause set in motion.

Decide upon your own inner quest, a quest that excites you and drives you through the desire of what you want out of life or through dissatisfaction with your present situation to get what you want. You will be motivated either by moving *towards* a goal or moving *away from* pain. So either get dissatisfied to make things happen or, even better, get proactive and work towards your goals.

A concept I will be exploring in more detail later is the theory of the two halves of the brain. It is now accepted that the left side of the brain prefers to analyse, break things down into constituent parts, is logical and relies on facts and reasoning, and the right prefers to synthesize by putting parts together to form the whole, see things as they are, relies on intuition and instinct and is creative and imaginative. This has massive implications for how we are motivated in life because a left brained person will be motivated by completing logical, detailed, factual and structured tasks. Whereas a more right brained person will be motivated by the opportunity to be creative, practical and imaginative.

Each side of the brain experiences the world differently.

Moving forward throughout the rest of the book I will be setting tasks that appeal to both sides of the brain - do all the exercises and think about which ones you prefer. From this you should consider if you are motivated more by left or right brained activities and consider how that influences the way you feel about home, work and life in general.

To summarise complete the following table and consider once again what really motivates you.

Motivation	Description	What & How it motivates you
Pain	What dissatisfaction motivates you?	
Pleasure	What pleasure or goals motivate you?	
Stick	What criticism motivates you?	
Carrot	What praise and recognition?	
Extrinsic	What externally motivates you?	
Intrinsic	What internally motivates you?	
Physiological	What physiological needs motivate you?	
Social, Love or Belonging	What social and group needs motivate you?	
Cognitive	What decision-making, problem solving needs?	
Emotional	What makes you feel good or bad? What do you react too?	
Self Esteem	What status, achievement, recognition needs?	

Conative	What form of control motivates you?	
Internal Self Concept	What is your internal view of yourself and how does that influence you?	
External Self Concept	What is your external view of yourself and how does that influence you?	
Homeostatic	What motivates you to stay static?	
Change	What change motivates you?	
Left Brain	How do your left-brain needs motivate you?	
Right Brain	How do your right-brain needs motivate you?	
Self-Actualization	How does realizing the self and potential motivate you?	
Spiritual	How do your spiritual needs for meaning motivate you?	

Each life lived throughout the generations has been an epic tale and the magnificent achievements of individuals, groups, peoples, races, and civilizations can be found within our illustrious history. It is realizing our own vast potential to become all we can be and understanding that this journey starts right now - you are a hero (heroine) about to embark on your life's quest. Find your sense of purpose and begin your inner quest through the spirit to become and the soul to be. The search for meaning begins by taking accountability for this life, no excuses, no lies, no deception, to be true to our self, to our own code and way of life, to live with passion in pursuit of the vision - the Super You.

Your inner quest has begun - let's cry together to live, to love, to learn, to become all we can be!

Life Changing Questions

What are you extrinsically motivated by?
What are you intrinsically motivated by?
What do you want from life?
What pain do you associate with not achieving what you want?
What pleasure do you associate with achieving what you want?
How can you relate your life to the motivational theories?
What is your sense of purpose? What is driving you?

"The future belongs to those who believe in the beauty of dreams."
- Eleanor Roosevelt

...and so out of darkness came the light until the paths of indecision and contradiction became open. Across the landscape of the mind a subterranean world of conditioning and deeply instilled beliefs, values, habits as if programmed for all time.

'One must choose to go right or left, forwards or backwards, and realize that one's choice dictates what one's life will become.'

Summary

1. Motivation is an internal state that, when activated, changes behaviour through a desire, need or want.

2. We are all motivated by pain or pleasure.

3. Some people are more extrinsically motivated while others intrinsically.

4. Maslow suggested we are motivated by a hierarchy of needs.

5. Taking proactive measures in life will result in a consistent motivation which is driven by individual meaning, aspiration and achievement.

6. You need to have an innate sense of purpose and a goal.

7. We are motivated either towards a goal or away from dissatisfaction.

8. Consider what side of the brain you use the most and how that affects your motivation

9. Take accountability for your own life's inner quest and become all you can be

   "The purpose of life is a life of purpose." - Robert Byrne

Reality Check

In the prologue the key message was 'why are you here?' It explored through the speaker the importance of being positive and optimistic, the importance of values and to recognize the vast potential you have.

Chapter 1 starts by exploring your subconscious map of the world and how we are all conditioned by life experiences. It helps you to consider your mindset by considering the premises upon which you base your life. The chapter also suggests we should make the most of the something we have, that life is a continual cycle of being and becoming and we should strive to become all that we can be. Life is a gift so we should make the most of that gift and hence get our internal maps right.

Chapter 2 suggests that we have a choice in life - we can embrace it and take part or observe and deny life, that we can be an optimist or pessimist, that we can choose our own destiny and become everything we choose to be.

Chapter 3 explores different theories of motivation enabling us to consider what really motivates us so that we can establish a list of the 'whats' we really want in life. It also makes us consider how we are motivated by moving towards pleasure or away from dissatisfaction or pain.

It also explores that we are motivated by the way we use our brain, which has significant impact upon what turns us on and how we approach our life and what literally turns or switches us off.

So where is this going? I want to inspire you to take part in the great cycle of life...for you to take accountability for your life, and to make it a tale in the making.

'Men are disturbed, not by things that happen, but by their opinion of the things that happen.' - Epictetus

Interlude 1: The Inner Guide

"A man who thinks he knows something knows he knows nothing at all." - Anonymous

The scene: The Magician faces the crowd outside a temple with the sea in the background of a serene landscape. Waves gently lap across the shore as the breeze moves in a swirl of mist and change. The Academy listens in respectful silence and anticipation.

'O my people, how I yearn for today, and every day to be today, where art thou?'

Would thee listen to me astounded by the sound of my voice that echoes upon these distant shores? Would thee hear sirens playing with the beating of thy heart like a distant drum, or is this a hollow song that will only end in the silence of thy judging minds?

How I wish to touch and caress your soul, freeing you from the chains of yesterday and tomorrow. In that we all feel the wholeness of this present moment and future present moments by touching the break of day and fall of the leaves at night. There we can find human nature in the feeling of being surrounded by nature, the waterfall in the distance, the waves lapping across the sands, the sun warming the skin. How beautiful is this vision of the present day all around us?

What is your motivation for living? Why bother, children of the world? The evidence before the court is that you are all showing feelings of an almost human nature. Together we have left Eden but you had to go your own way from naturalness to socialness to only individuals in loneliness, diversity and uncertainty. Are you alone in your loneliness?

Who did you follow to find me? Who brought you to me?

Is it your search to find meaning, hope, charity in an endless journey of becoming or will you find reckoning in that your senses lie to you, nothing is, everything is idea, so you observe and simply be. A passer-by in history.

O how you find me with the will to a greater love which starts through the 'I' in you. What great 'I' would that be my fellow compatriots? The self cries out to you in vanity to be recognized, to be nurtured, to be realized. What more could one ask for in knowing thyself and in loving the self. For what greater motivation can there be for living?

Would I be a fool to lead you on, for in this fire the baptism of the soul is in having the spirit to love thyself.

O spirit, have I found you wanting or found you waiting across this world, across the solemn sea, across the stars in the night sky? How far can you wait if not through ageless years - leaving your naturalness behind? Forming complexes and leaving thy spirit afar. O spirit, awaken, awaken some more to realize this life evermore.

> *O spirit that awakens me awaken me whole*
> *In that no Devil or demon can take my soul.*
> *Keep me fresh from the plunder,*
> *Away from the hordes,*
> *For this striving for life gives me endless rewards.*

> *And I'll go on a wandering,*
> *   A wandering on my way*
> *To find loves great adventures*
> *   Hopefully today,*
> *And I'll walk across the bridges*
> *   to my own infinity*
> *Hoping that my feet*
> *   Will grace Galilee.*

O spirit that possesses me possess me some more
Giving me the will to love that opens all doors,
Saving me from violence,
Safe from remorse,
In that I will feel the rhythm of the universal force.

And I'll continue a searching,
            A searching for my self
Where else can lie true richness
            And wealth,
And I'll carry on a thinking
            Of my golden harmony
Where in an ideal world
            There would be you and me.

O spirit that surrounds me surround me with grace,
Enlightening my mind and giving me a place,
Far away from the selfishness,
Away from the greed,
So that I can sow the reaping harvest of love's seed.

And I'll forever keep on loving,
            Loving all things,
Feeling all the joyful freshness
            That life brings
And I'll always remember you
            Shaping my path
And giving me the power
            To endlessly laugh.

O spirit all around me continue to stay,
For there are tales to be told as we carry on our way,
A way for the living,
A way for us all,
A way for the human spirit to evolve evermore!

I stand before you like a mirror - the mirror and the 'I' in you. O and who brought you here but the 'I' yourself who is all knowing and all seeing. Brought by coincidence and curiosity in meaningful disarray. Confused, fallen, re-born....O awaken to your true feelings, awaken the ultimate power within.

O spirits now heed me no more for I am a shadow of my true self and that shadow guides me as I wander, as I wonder would you all not sooner, in life and in death, become all that you can be. This great willing will will an age for a new millennium - a new people who have found their true self.

And so I have to take my leave, to live, to love, to learn, to life forever evermore!'

Chapter 4: The Soul & The Spirit

Santa Spirita, breather, life,
Beyond the light, lighter than light,
Beyond the flames of hell - joyous,
    leaping easily above hell;
Beyond Paradise - perfumed solely
    with mine own perfume;
Including all life on earth - touching, including
    God - including Savior and Satan;
Ethereal, pervading all - for, without me,
    what were all? What were God?
Essence of forms - life of the real identities,
    permanent, positive, namely unseen,
Life of the great round world, the sun and the stars,
    and of man - I, the General Soul.
- Walt Whitman

So we know what we want in life and we have explored what motivation is and the different theories of motivation and how they apply to our life. Let's focus on the bigger picture from a holistic point of view, which appeals to the creative right side of the brain.

In the beginning there was something - a something that meant there could be no nothing. Across the great plains within the landscape of something lay vast opportunities for all life to grow. In a fleeting glimpse upon the horizon a solitary soul walked towards the west, shining bright consistent endeavour upon the sands. This soul crossed mountain, hill and brook until it found a garden of contentment. There the soul rested touched by a heavenly grace that beckoned infinity. Years passed and the soul was, is and was to be again. Then a bright burning blazed upon the morning sky with boundless energy. It was a spirit born with life's fire craving adventure and excitement. The spirit raged across the landscape conquering each corner of the earth until eventually it came upon the sacred garden.

For spirit met soul and soul met spirit.

Each carefully inspected the other unsure of their differences, secure in their similarities. They talked of their beginnings, their conquests and their passions feeling a great coming together with the weight of destiny upon their shoulders. Love entwined the spirit and the soul until they became like one, moved like one, talked like one, felt like one. In that moment it was like time itself stopped beating to a still as the lovers caressed the light of the day and the shadows of the night. Filling the sky with kisses of life stretched upon the drifting rhythm of the breeze, delicately and desiringly in union with the fall and the rise of each civilization. But time had not stopped as the soul eternal, 'the essence to be,' danced with the spirit of inner fire, 'the will to become'.

The spirit that created passion and splendour within the history of mankind had lived beyond the measure of its mortality, finally passing over across the wastelands until spirit was no more. There was the tragedy for the eternal soul to be left with only the memory of the love once held, once consumed. Love was all - the spirit was gone. Humanity's sorrow echoed upon the landscape of evermore life. The soul lamented the inconceivable loss of love.

Ages passed and he who watched over all things realized a question in answer, 'Where lies a soul without a spirit or a spirit without a soul? The essence and the realm. There lies the soul cause and the soul eventuality within the fiery spirit of man, that of evermore life.'

What has motivated man in the past?

In the beginning there was something as opposed to nothing because something cannot come from nothing. Whether that something came from a God or Gods or through the interaction of existing chemicals in space there had to be something. The something we know is life on Earth.

It's amazing to think that dinosaurs roamed the Earth for hundreds of millions years before the evolution of mankind, especially considering the limited numbers of years we have of recorded history.

So what motivated man to create, to build, to multiply? Was it out of a total disregard for his kind, to plunder, to destroy, to complete dominance over the species – perhaps not, for mankind has ensured his own perseverance and survival in attempting to leave a legacy upon the landscape. When mankind hunted in the age of the dinosaur there is evidence of creativity through cave paintings and rituals to the Gods. Our earliest ancestors lived in Africa 2.5 million years ago (Home Habilis) and through evolution from man apes we developed into the Homo Sapien. Rock engravings can be found in Australia dating back 40000 ago years with figures of people and animals made out of clay by mammoth hunters from 27000 BC. It was around 10000 BC that mankind clothed himself to survive the ice age using fur from the woolly mammoth and other hunted animals. Can you imagine that same man within his clan sitting gazing into a sunset after satisfyingly bringing down a mammoth that would feed his family for months? Looking towards the sky wondering why we are here? What is our purpose? What can I teach my kids? By 8000 BC mankind had learned to grow crops and raised animals for food and communities started to develop. In Jericho the first town developed at around 2000 people. By 7000 BC the first recorded tools were used in the near east giving significant rise to ancient technology. And how man explored to find better ways of living, better places, better people!

By 5000 BC the first civilizations formed through the Sumerians, the Assyrians and Babylonians. Although it is rumored a groove ware people were civilized and became architects in Ireland, Britain and Scandinavia, building precise temples and houses in line with the light from Venus, showing an astounding knowledge of astronomy and technology for that time. Was it this group of people who later built Stonehenge and who travelled to the Middle-East to share their knowledge and wisdom? And who were the Atlanteans?

Across the Middle-East fortresses where built and burned to the ground with countless wars and civilization's re-discovery. Gods came and passed by like fashions upon the wind. By 3500 the Sumerians invented writing and the wheel. By 2900 BC Kings were established within the main Sumerian cities and by 2100 BC the magnificent city of UR was at the height of its power personified by the great Ziggurat to the moon God Nanna. Then the Assyrian empire for over a thousand years waged war with Babylon. King Hammurabi was the first King of Babylon in 1792 – 1750 BC essentially developing a fair way of living for all through what were the beginnings of fair and democratic laws. When King Nebuchadezzar II rebuilt Babylon he made one of the seven wonders of the world in the beautiful and creative hanging gardens of Babylon. What a wonderful exquisite site that must have been to behold across the barren landscape of Mesopotamia. How travellers would have marvelled at such a site.

During this time Egypt flourished from 5000 BC, with the first boats to have sails on the Nile by 4000 BC and early hieroglyphs by 3200 BC. The first pyramids were built from 2686 BC and the Sphinx and Great Pyramid were built at Giza in 2580 BC. The great flood in Noah's story took place in 2567 and the tale of Joseph and his Technicolor coat less than 4000 years ago. Moses as a baby was wrapped in a basket and pushed into the Nile in 1575 BC, to be found by the Pharoes wife to be given good grace, and to grow up in good fortune accepted by the Egyptians and who held his own people, the Israelites, as slaves. Moses eventually freed his people under God's guidance escaping across the Red Sea to Mount Sinai to receive the Ten Commandments. The commandments that conditioned man what not to do.

At this time ancient populations flourished and grew at a staggering rate. Man's motivation at that time? To survive and provide for one's family, to develop their standard of living through discovery of new technology, to worship God or Gods with real meaning in life, to be creative through art in its earliest form through figures, paintings, statues, and temples, to expand territories through farming, through growing communities and towns, through war and domination. What was a time of meaning through religion and unity through war was soon to become a time of illumination and reasoning throughout the Greek world.

In 900 BC the great warlike city of Sparta was founded. In 700 Homer completed the tales of the Iliad and the Odyssey, still believed to be based on real events; the myth of Troy and Achilles, the voyage of Odysseus, and the many more Greek legends and tales of the Gods of Olympus. By 508 BC democracy ruled in Athens and the Greeks built mighty temples to their Gods. Pericles built the Parthenon in 447BC to 438BC and the Acropolis was built also at that time. Greek culture was defined through the creativity of its architecture, its vases, its actors through drama at amphitheaters, through its great poets and the classical philosophers of Socrates, Plato and Aristotle, and the beginnings of competitive sport through the Olympics. Alexander the Great of Macedonia, educated by Aristotle, built a great empire spanning out deep into Asia, which eventually became part of the Roman Empire.

For when Alexander saw he had no more worlds to conquer he wept.

Rome was founded in 753 BC with the Roman Republic established in 509 BC. After Alexander, came Rome's dominance, the Punic wars developed and raged from 264 to 146 BC when Rome and Carthage battled. Hannibal almost took Rome with his 35,000 men and 37 elephants, which he managed to cross the Alps with – a feat of pure courage and belief in cause. The Roman army went on to build a magnificent empire across Europe and into Britain, building roads and viaducts with such magnificence along the way. Then there was Rome itself, the dream that was Rome, with decadence shrouded in beautiful arches and architecture. O and how the Coliseum burned brightly with its roaring crowd cheering the hero of the moment. The splendour that was Rome, the ideal that was Rome, the roads that all lead to Rome. What is Rome for you in this modern day and age?

How Rome has taught us that nothing lasts forever for in Ad 40 the unthinkable happened the barbarian tribes of the north sacked the great city. How true could this be in our lifetimes when not only self destruction through nuclear war threatens to devastate modern civilization but also the fear of natural disasters through global warming or a modern day ice age or through a devastating Tsunami?

Oh how there has been pain and murder, rape and pillage, wrongdoings and destruction along the way, but there has also been enlightenment and creativity, sport and recreation, art and architecture, love and war, sorrow and darkness, happiness and light.

Some would say the essence lies in the struggle, not in the victory.

For did not Jesus, the son of the hand of God, the human man, prove that through self-sacrifice for all mankind. Was the whole story of Christ a real myth and an archetypal reality? The conquering of good over evil, the power of belief and the will to love one's fellow man. The Roman legacy and the legend of Jesus lived on and in 325 at the council of Niceae it was decided upon whether Christ was the Son of God or purely a mortal man. The new found Christian church through the beliefs of Saul decided that Christ was immortal and a deity, banishing all pagan beliefs of Mother Nature and the fact that Christ was mortal. What an achievement the bible was to become, a man made legacy of history and Christ, written by man not God. Man's actual account, doctored to fit with the right regime and propaganda and any other chapters to be burnt or lost or to be called hearsay. How dare thee believe Christ had a wife or child, which then cleared the way for a male dominated culture for the next 2000 years.

But most women were conditioned by circumstance not to expect any different and man to expect domination.

In the next thousand years a greater myth was born of King Arthur and the Holy Grail within the new holy land. A small island that was to become Great Britain, a country so small that, for its size, to conquer and colonize the unknown world was some mean feat. What a tale of complete archetypal significance to every single person's lives with the figures of Arthur, Merlin, Lancelot and the Kingdom of Camelot. The faithful King - a boy who becomes a King who becomes a Knight who builds a Kingdom who is betrayed by his Queen and best Friend; a story of heroism and tragedy, rich in archetypal subconscious figures that form part of our collective psyche; a tale that symbolizes the duality of life's choices and the reality of modern day life.

Then came the crusades when the Muslim Turks banned Christians from the city of Jerusalem and so started the wars of belief fighting belief. The first crusade was in 1096 and Jerusalem was captured in 1099. What was mankind's motivation then? To travel the whole of Europe to conquer in the name of a greater belief, in the name of good, in the name of God? Can you imagine facing the city of Jerusalem, swords and armour glistening in the night sky convinced that it was your right as a Christian to fight for your cause in the holy war? The Knights Templar excavated the Temple of Solomon, son of David, to find a great treasure (perhaps even the Ark of the Covenant), a treasure still hidden this day in so many different rumoured locations, Ethiopia, Roslyn, America. The Knights Templar found great riches that led to great power that was eventually crushed through the King of France on Friday 13th 1307, the freemasons retaining the secrets of Harim, the key architect of the Temple of Solomon, and perhaps the hidden treasure of King Solomon's mines.

Then followed the age of discovery, with the fall of Constantinople ending the traces of the Roman Empire in 1453. Printing was developed in the 1450's and books became available to those who could read. Columbus set sail from Spain in 1492, and the Renaissance reached its height in 1500 as Leonardo Da Vinci paints the Mona Lisa in 1503 and Michelangelo paints the Sistine Chapel in the Vatican. In 1543 Copernicus suggested that the Earth revolved around the sun at the center of our Solar System - what a total paradigm shift at that time.

The colonization of the America's followed in the late 16th Century, the French naming the north Canada, the English with Sir Walter Raleigh setting up Jamestown, swiftly to be followed by the Pilgrim Fathers and the Spanish to the South with Florida and Mexico. Then followed the slave trade, wars of independence and revolution in a time of chaotic uprising for the rights of the people epitomized in 1776 by the 'Declaration of Independence' July 4th creating the United States, and followed by the French revolution of 1789.

Then came the Enlightenment when people's new ideas about personal freedom, religious beliefs and politics emerged. At this time great scholars, philosophers and scientists put forward original ideas in print for all to read influencing the hearts and minds of the people. At the same time a new empire was being built with the British colonization of Canada, Australia, Asia, and Africa. The last great empire.

In 1859 Charles Darwin wrote the Origin of the Species with the theory of Evolution - a theory so groundbreaking he was ridiculed in his own time.

And how the world has evolved, civilization has evolved; we have evolved through the spirit of man.

And so to modern times with the unification of the countries within Europe, Italy and Germany, which was to be swiftly followed by two brutal world wars. Can you imagine being called up to go to war at the tentative age of 18 and actually believing you were going on a great adventure to find oneself deep in trenches of mud and fire? Expected to go over those trenches straight in to enemy fire to win what? Perhaps 10 yards for freedom. Who would doubt the courage of those that died and fought on the poppy fields, legends in their own right? And do we remember?

After the war came a time of unity and collective identity through community values, people looked out for one another. The period after the war was one of high employment particularly in the UK after the introduction of the Social Democratic Welfare State and government intervention. This was a great shift from the great depression between the wars when employment and the poverty gap were high, with the 1950's and 60's being the golden years of industry, and family life offering certainty and stability.

But how times have changed with diverse living arrangements, uncertainty, greater choice of consumer goods, globalization and a shift from collective identity and community values to the very individualistic world that we now live in. With the knowledge explosion of the 1980's we now live as experts, being able to obtain information of all kinds of subjects never dreamed possible. How social arrangements have changed for example where the father held power as the patriarchal father figure through coercive power. We now see diverse living arrangements and what was perceived as normal is now challenged by each individual's freedom to choose who they want to be, what they want to be and how they want to live. Our modern day freedoms give us greater choice and diversity. For here lies the dilemma. In the past that choice was made for us, we had to work in the coal mines, we had to go to war, we had to bring our children up and be a good housewife. And we had deep meaning through the certainty of our God, the Sun, or Yahweh, or Zeus, but how that has changed from life filled churches being a way of life to modern day ghost alleys within the house of God. Have we deserted God or do we now have new Gods? Or are old wrongs never to be forgotten with an ongoing war between Gods like old crusades?

This is only a glimpse at history - a history we are still being conditioned by. Can I ask, what do you really think of this world? For mankind's history is a tale in the making, this evolution has developed into the 21st Century and as sentient beings we exist on a physical, mental, emotional and spiritual level. As technology has become widely available we can all be experts through the Internet with information on every subject thought possible. This allows the 21st Century man the opportunity to become all he can be. With greater knowledge also comes greater responsibility through choice but unfortunately for most people pre-conditioning from their life and history means that they feel their choice has already been made. They live in the grey twilight of a pre-conditioned and reactive world without both the spirit to survive and become, and a soul offering meaning to their life.

As mankind has removed himself from the teleological, cosmological and ontological arguments in the belief in God and divine meaning, innate sense of purpose in the 21st Century becomes the search for the lost ark. In modern cosmopolitan cities and ivory towns, mankind rushes to meet technological deadlines as if competing in a race. Unfortunately along the way mankind has lost a deep religious background that offered immortality in the afterlife. This loss of religion and belief has intriguing effects in the case of psychiatric illnesses and personality disorders. In fact it is mankind's alignment to his myth and the loss of that mythological ambiguity that creates deep neuroses and complexes. In ancient times for example man worshipped the Sun, hunted and naturally reproduced. This was the only meaning needed which led to a relaxed way of life, stress free and a divine inner contentment. Compare that to modern day life with business, relationships, fashion, society, culture, laws, conformity, and conditioning.

Science in the 20th/21st Century has replaced religion and the individual person has evolved to become greater than the following herd. It is this loss of meaning; this not understanding why we are here that creates a void of darkness or emptiness in our lives. Throughout history mankind has formed law tables based on a morality of dualism. The motivation or reason can then be classified between this and that, good and evil, right and wrong, positive and negative. These classifications are a man made dialogue for the explanation, definition and understanding of our thoughts, feelings and actions. However, to truly understand motivation and enhance our life and other people's, we have to embrace dualism to improve our state of mind and accept it by learning from experience. Our state of mind should have no negative, wrong or evil motivation to achieve our desired goals. If you take yourself back through time to the first men and women who walked the Earth – what right or wrong would there have been then? This is mankind in a natural state of mind not filled with historical opinions, society's judgement, or culture's conformity, all of which have developed an unbalanced psyche of disorder and neurotic illness for many people.

The soul guides the spirit and the spirit guides the soul.

This is the ambiguity we have in our lives that most people fail to embrace.

For the soul wants to be and the spirit wants to become, hence the spirit lives through achievement as the spirit of man and the soul takes on the spiritual essence of being. It is the ability to live life knowing the depth of our soul by finding spiritual inner contentment, which gives us inner peace and balancing that with the fire of our spirit to become something in life through the continual development of becoming all we can be.

It is establishing deep inner reason and meaning and then moving towards our goal with that sense of purpose, combining the needs of both the soul and the spirit. Real motivation comes from a sense of being to a sense of becoming and then back to a sense of being through a singular state of positivity and a striving to be what we are, merely natural, within the essence of being and the realm of becoming.

This is where duality begins and it is having an appreciation of dualism in life to be able to balance the essence and the realm. Below is not saying Natural Man is right, good and positive while Complex man is not, it is purely an example of the opposites and hence our dualistic world.

This	That
Natural Man	Complex Man
Right	Wrong
Good	Evil
Positive	Negative
Introvert	Extrovert
Feelings	Thoughts
Internal	External
Being	Becoming

Embracing
The Soul Will
The Soul Eventuality

One thing is sure: we can never go back to Eden and we can never be reborn – same difference. However it is the balance between this and that, which is the end goal. That is the striving of the human spirit, which is the Soul's Will and Soul's Eventuality. 'Solve Coagula' could simply explain life; one needs to be broken down to be reborn because with all endings come new beginnings. It is the bad things that happen as well as the good that shape life. It is an appreciation of the part that these bad happenings play in sculpting our lives and embracing them with a positive vigour to learn and spiritually grow and enable us to find the balance.

Now to promote discovery and identify our deep internal motivation we shall venture back through time again. There we can appreciate or associate our inner meaning or where our inner motivation came from.

Hannibal Scenario

Imagine you are Hannibal back in Roman times. The century is 200BC. Hannibal lives in Carthage off the North coast of Africa. Now as we know Hannibal unbelievably crossed the Mediterranean, travelled through Spain and crossed the Alps with an army of elephants. He stormed Italy and defeated the Romans before settling in Verona. Hannibal never took Rome, however the achievement speaks for itself.

Before you head for Rome to conquer the city and before you crossed the Alps what would your main considerations be?

Once you have completed that write down how you would feel before attempting such an escapade.

We will return to your answers later. Imagine what your life would have been like if you lived in these particular time periods:

- Biblical times when Moses parted the sea.

- Babylon, with the Tower of Babel reaching up to the sky and the hanging gardens of Babylon.

- The Egyptian pyramids and the sphinx at Giza.

- The Greek Delphi and Acropolis.

- The Roman Coliseum and Pantheon.

- The Vikings voyage across the Atlantic.

- Medieval times with Arthur Pen Dragon and Merlin at Camelot.

- Renaissance Italy with Michelangelo, Leonardo da Vinci and Raphael.

- Or any other period of history that appeals to you.

Now you have completed this close your eyes and imagine which generation or era you feel you truly belonged to. Perhaps if reincarnation really does happen you have led several lives already. However for this exercise choose a time period and create these things with your imagination in detail.

Where do you live?

What do you look like?

What is your lifestyle?

What is your place in society?

What are your beliefs?

What are your motivation and goals in life?

Which era do you really feel connected to, is it one or several or all of them?

In answer to the questions do you look similar to what you look like now? Or are you different, stronger, richer, and better looking? Are your beliefs similar to now or are they of higher integrity, purpose, and cause? Do you live at the same standard within society or is your place of higher standing? Finally are your goals and motivation different to what they are now? What does this all tell you about yourself?

Do you feel a deep similarity to those times and the here and now? Because it was the same man, with the same unanswered questions as it is today? Deliberating over similar issues as we congress today. It is the feeling or weight of history that we cannot escape because we as individuals have been sculpted by our past and the history of the world. We truly belong to the present moment however the narrative of the past is etched already upon our souls. It is this link to mankind that leads us to feelings of deja vu, the mysterious, coincidences, and the deep paradoxical world of the unknown.

But it is also appreciation of life as life is a lesson in appreciation.

Everything in this life should hold some form of fascination giving us a feeling and belief that there is more to life than our existence being down to chance. How many experiences in life have you had that you would live your life over again for? How many experiences have you had where you have been elated or happy beyond measure? When you wake up the morning, who is responsible for you feeling like that every day of your life?

Write down some of the beautiful things or experiences you have had in life. Perhaps you have been to Rome and seen the Sistine Chapel, or been awestruck by a landscape within the Alps or fallen deeply in love with a beautiful person.

Can we then question the universal pattern of life?

You shape your own destiny and your destiny shapes you.

For the measure is found in the depth of our soul and the fire of our spirit.

I sit here, and there is not a single thing in the room that does not hold some kind of fascination, for in true appreciation if you take in everything around you, the shapes, the colours, the smells, the sound and the touch then how can you deny the pattern? Everything around you is beautiful, it is perfection, and it is understanding the part that everyone has to play in the pattern.

> *"Somewhere within us, no matter how lost or confused we might be there is something within which has foresight and resources which are often hidden from consciousness but which can divine what direction and what choices to make. The magician does not come when he is called. He comes in the form of disturbing dreams or in the guise of a meeting with another person who turns out to be significant as a catalyst on the journey.*
>
> *The guide appears as a hunch, the book one accidentally reads, chance visit by a friend, all are the handiwork of the inner guide your spiritual teacher."* - The Mythic Tarot

Who is the one person that you talk to the most in one day or in your whole life?

Yourself. Every minute of every day. And would you say that you talk to yourself either in a positive confident manner or at times in a very negative and self doubting one? And perhaps sometimes you talk to yourself in a higher voice? The voice that seems to know exactly what is the right thing to do?

Our self-talk, along with our thoughts, the language we use and our physiology will determine the outcome. Focusing on the mind...

Your *conscious* mind is the you that exists everyday. Your *conscious* mind is objective and thinking. It is the part which makes the decisions, it identifies information through the senses, categorizes and compares the information, analyses and then decides on a course of action.

Your *conscious* mind is your conscience as well because it makes the decisions; therefore it has the choice to be truthful or to lie.

Your *subconscious* mind is like a data bank of information, which stores every single piece of information or experience from your life. Your conscious mind only recalls what is essential and important and takes all the minor details for granted. Because of the way our *conscious* mind is educated it means that the pattern or fascination discussed above passes most people by because most people are too busy being busy or too involved with the flow of their life. We remember the significant things in our life in what we associate to be significant to ourselves. The *subconscious* mind is totally subjective in that it will obey and follow the conscious mind's emotions, thoughts and feelings by matching the correct behaviours. The *subconscious* mind likes to regulate things and will attempt to keep things consistent in the sense it will pull you back to your comfort zone. In fact it is homeostatic in that it will keep you thinking and acting consistently with past behaviour and actions.

The magnificent thing with the *subconscious* mind is that it will make the things you think about the most happen.

'A man becomes what he thinks about the most!' - Ralph Waldo Emerson

In a sense your expectations of life will become your realities and your subconscious will help to make those expectations become true.

'If you think you can, you can
If you think you can't, you're right.'
Henry Ford

The last part is the *greater subconscious* mind; this is the you that you talk to in your head. It has been referred to as Infinite Intelligence by Napolean Hill, the Oversoul by Ralph Waldo Emerson, and the Collective Unconscious by Carl Gustav Jung. The *greater subconscious* mind is your source of inspiration; it brings you ideas out of the blue and the experiences or coincidences you need at the right time in your life. It is the one that brings you insights, taking you to the right place at the right time.

This is your inner guide, guardian angel, inner spirit or daemon, your genius. It is your calling.

The unconscious power that looks after us appears to offer guidance and wisdom touching the spheres of the mind, imagination, heart and body suggesting potential skills and creative abilities yet to manifest. It is the upsurge of energy and intuition of new opportunities and unexplored possibilities. Everyone has an innate calling and reason that their unique person is here and it is tapping into that potential and realizing that accidents are part of the pattern and help to fulfil it.

There can be no more motivation than that fleeting glimpse of everything we can be. It is the Soul Image and Soul Eventuality that we help to create. A sense of belonging to a higher order of destiny, the dream should never be relinquished. It is not that anything is possible but everything that is possible we help to create.

Mankind has created and built wonders in the world and by being in touch with our **greater subconscious** it will help to create marvels in our own life. Within us this second person holds the key to our deep sense of purpose and our self-esteem.

> "*Soon after this fantasy another figure rose out of the unconscious. He developed out of the Elijah figure. I called him Philemon. Philemon was a pagan and brought with him an Egypto-Hellenic atmosphere with a Gnostic colouration. His figure first appeared to me in the following dream.*
>
> *There was a blue sky, like the sea, covered not by clouds but by flat brown clods of earth. It looked as if the clods were breaking apart and the blue water of the sea were becoming visible between them. But the water was the blue sky. Suddenly there appeared from the right a winged being sailing across the sky. I saw that it was an old man with the horns of a bull. He held a bunch of four keys, one of which*

he clutched as if he were about to open a lock. He had the wings of the kingfisher with its characteristic colours.

Since I did not understand this dream image, I painted it in order to impress it upon my memory. During the days when I was occupied with the painting, I found in my garden, by the lakeshore, a dead kingfisher! I was thunderstruck, for kingfishers are quite rare in the vicinity of Zurich and I have never since found a dead one was recently dead – at most, two or three days and showed no external injuries.

Philemon and other figures of my fantasies brought home to me the crucial insight that there are things in the psyche which I do not produce, but which produce themselves and have their own life.

Philemon represented a force which was not myself. In my fantasies I held conversations with him, and he said things which I had not consciously thought. For I observed clearly that it was he who spoke, not I.

He said I treated thoughts as if I generated them myself, but in his view thoughts were like animals in the forest, or people in a room, or birds in the air and added "If you should see people in a room, you would not think that you had made those people, or that you were responsible for them." It was he who taught me psychic objectivity, the reality of the psyche. Through him the distinction was clarified between myself and the object of my thought. He confronted me in an objective manner, and I understood that there is something in me which can say things that I do not know and do not intend, things which may even be directed towards me.

Psychologically, Philemon represented superior insight. He was a mysterious figure to me. At times he seemed to me quite real, as if he were a living personality. I went walking up and down the garden with him, and to me he was what Indians call a guru." - C.G.Jung – Memories, Dreams, Reflections. Chap: Confrontation with the Unconscious.

The greater conscious mind works within the pattern and only when we are open to it will we notice the insights it brings. The more open we are to believe positively that good things will happen in life and that the world conspires to do us good then we will be more open to notice its gifts.

Solutions come intuitively, through chance encounters, through our dreams, through daydreaming and time out in solitude, by asking questions to our greater self. The greater subconscious upholds the truth and guides us if we are willing to listen to our inner voice and purpose of the heart.

Clairvoyants communicate with guardian angels and guiding spirits and the Greeks believed that we were given an inner guide to take us along the journey; a journey to improve life with each life.

Are you improving life this time around? Are you developing further?

Let's now go back to Hannibal. What considerations did you make before setting out on such an adventure?

To plan the conquest in detail with beginning, middle, and end?
To set clear, achievable goals?
To start with the end in mind?
To create passion in the troops?
To visualise success?
To have passion and belief in the cause?
To recognize that you are in control of your own destiny?
How would you feel? Scared, exhilarated, nervous, confident, doubtful?

Hannibal's self motivation enabled him to achieve an exceptional feat but to be successful and to have that innate internal motivation we have to recognize exactly how we think and feel about the project, about our own conquests and life.

It is how we feel about a thing that motivates us!

And through our inner guide we can feel a holistic direction that is full of personal meaning. It is being in touch with our soul and with nature, it is being and becoming ad infinitum. The Essence and the Realm.

> For I have learned
> To look on nature, not as in the hour
> Of thoughtless youth, but hearing oftentimes
> The still, sad music of humanity,
> Not harsh nor grating, though of ample power
> To chasten and subdue. And I have felt
> A presence that disturbs me with joy
> Of elevated thoughts; a sense sublime
> Of something far more deeply interfused,
> Whose dwelling is the light of setting suns,
> And the round ocean , and the living air,
> And the blue sky, and the mind of man,
> A motion and a spirit that impels
> All thinking things, all objects of thought
> And rolls through all things.
> - William Wordsworth

We all have a greater destiny.

Everything happens for a reason.

You shape your destiny and your destiny shapes you.

The soul guides the spirit and the spirit guides the soul.

Life Changing Questions

What has motivated you in the past?
What have been your past achievements?
What have been your past disappointments?
Who has been in control of your past experiences?
What meaningful coincidences have you had in your life?
How do you feel about life and what you want?

How are you finding the Essence of Being?
How are you using the fire within your spirit of the Realm to Become?
What is your greater purpose?

> *"The whole course of human history may depend on a change of heart in one solitary and even humble individual - for it is in the solitary mind and soul of the individual that the battle between good and evil is waged and ultimately won or lost." - M. Scott Peck*

> 'Look inside yourself to see how deep your soul goes; how far have you fallen from heaven, once an angel of the Lord lost and searching? How far have you flown from your true self? How far have you wandered from your own inner uniqueness and beauty, from your own conscience, once your highest hope now forgotten in endless days? Remember the feeling of being alive, living, loving, learning and saying yes to life, yes, yes, yes — remember my sweet cherubim.'

Summary

1. The soul guides the spirit and the spirit guides the soul.

2. It was the same man in the past, with the same unanswered questions as it is today. Your feelings of déjà vu leave you sometimes with the feeling that we have been here before. It was the same man that came before us, feeling the same things, thinking the same thoughts and through the wonderful creations in the world that man has made it gives us a glimpse of everything we can be.

3. You shape your own destiny and your destiny shapes you.

4. Your greater subconscious acts like an inner guide helping you to realize your calling.

   + Your inner guide shapes your future and if you are willing to tap into your unconscious you can feel an internal locus that provides an innate sense of purpose and individual destiny.

- Giving you an appreciation of the dualism within life embracing the Soul Will and Soul Eventuality.

5. A man becomes what he thinks about the most.

6. It is how you feel about a thing that motivates you.

7. What is your materialistic motivation to become or achieve? What is your spiritual motivation to find the essence of your being?

"Man is the measure of all things." - Protagoras

Chapter 5: The Will to Love

"My beloved speaks to me:
Arise, my love, my fair one
and come away;
for now the winter is past,
the rain is over and gone.
The flowers appear on the earth;
the time of singing has come,
and the voice of the turtle dove
is heard in our land.
The fig tree puts forth its figs,
and the vines are in blossom;
they give forth fragrance.
Arise, my love, my fair one,
And come away.'

Set me as a seal upon your heart,
As a seal upon your arm;
for love is strong as death,
passion fierce as the grave.
Its flashes are flashes of fire, a
raging flame.
Many waters cannot quench love,
neither can floods drown it.
If one offered for love
all the wealth of one's house
it would be utterly scorned.
-        Song of Solomon
-        2.10 – 13:8.6.7

What have we established? That we are two people that are one, that our inner guide drives our inner destiny if we are willing to listen, and that we are part of some kind of collective mass psyche who has lived previous lives? (That's a bit far fetched, would you say?) The fact is though we do talk to ourselves every day, every hour, every minute and most people talk themselves down with self-criticism. If I were to ask you to answer the following question truthfully – do you really listen to your greater self – the self that wants the best for you, the self that knows best and the self that does the right thing for the right reasons or do you drown out that higher voice to shape a lesser existence? To live an easier life? You have the choice in life to decide who you want to be and it is being able to channel positive energy to help you along your own inner quest to determine your own subterranean landscapes of the mind and life. Let's focus on where we can find that positive energy…

Once again I would like to take you back through history. I would like to resurrect one of the creators in the movement of positive motivation in my belief. This was Friedrich Nietzsche, who was born in Saxony in 1844.

Nietzsche became a Professor in his mid twenties, which at the time was unheard of. He became a philosopher and produced many books such as the Birth of Tragedy, Human All Too Human, The Gay Science, Beyond Good and Evil, and his most famous, Thus Spoke Zarathustra. He was influenced by the ideas of Schopenhauer and Wagner however he turned against both. It is within Nietzsche's philosophy that we shall journey next. Within Nietzsche's later work he invented four main themes that I would like to focus on and expand upon in relation to motivation. Now because I do not want to contradict myself I will stress I have not mentioned God and I do not want to be associated with Nietzsche's statement that God is dead. For the reader's purpose Nietzsche believed that there was no God and no life outside the existing one. His four main themes were the Will to Power, Ubermensh – interpreted as the Superman, Eternal Recurrence and the Tragedy of Life, which is the aesthetic understanding of life. From these life-affirming philosophies we can draw upon a source of inspiration. Now Schopenhauer regarded the will as the source of man's unhappiness and all evil on earth. Nietzsche's view of the will was in complete contrast to this; he regards it as the origin and source of man's strength. To be motivated, there has to be something within us driving us forwards. This may be a need, a desire, or an emotion that leads us to act. It is feelings within ourselves that create thoughts of inner direction and, more importantly, engaging our will to act. To will is to decide. Therefore it becomes a conscious decision (although perhaps at times based on subconscious feelings) to behave in a certain way. We will or our will shows a definite or deliberate intention.

Of the Thousand and One Goals

'A table of values hangs over every people. Behold, it is the table of its overcomings; behold, it is the voice of its will to power.

What it accounts hard it calls praiseworthy; what it accounts indispensable and hard it calls good; and that which relieves the greatest need, the rare, the hardest of all – it glorifies as holy.

Whatever causes it to rule and conquer and glitter, to the dread and envy of its neighbour, that it accounts the sublimest, the paramount, the evaluation and meaning of all things.

Truly, my brothers, if you only knew people's need and land and sky and neighbour, you could surely divine the law of its overcomings, and why it is upon this ladder that it mounts towards its highest hope.
- Fredriech Nietzsche - Thus Spoke Zarathustra

Taking the idea of the will further mankind has a will to survive like all animals, a will to achieve and create and a Will to Power in Nietzsche's words. Our will to power is the drive or inner motivation to become the superman or better man, overcoming oneself to further develop and improve.

Of Self Overcoming

And life itself told me this secret: 'Behold,' it said, 'I am that which must be overcome itself again and again.

'To be sure, you call it will to procreate or impulse towards a goal, towards the higher more distant, more manifold: but all this is one and one secret.

'I would rather perish than renounce this one thing; and truly, where there is perishing and falling of leaves, behold, there life sacrifices itself – for the sake of power!

'That I have to be struggle and becoming and goal and conflict of goals: ah, he who divines my will surely divines, too, along what crooked paths it has to go!' - Fredriech Nietzsche - Thus Spoke Zarathustra

Nietzsche claims 'only where there is life, there is also will: not will to life but....will to power. There is much that life esteems more highly than itself: But out of the esteeming itself speaks the will to power', the will to power being more than a striving to affect others or as a will to realize oneself. It is essentially a striving to transcend and perfect oneself; the desire to become all that we can be, which is to transcend the will to life or self-preservation.

This Will to Power we shall pursue because Mankind's one true source of motivation is the **Will to Love**, starting with the will to survive because of self-love – it is the decision not to curl up and die! Through our will to love ourselves we in fact choose life for ourselves and hence effort is exerted through the will to improve our lives. Within a safe environment and advanced society the will to love evolves dependent upon the self-need. The will to love comes from the driving force of self-love and with self-love at the core the will to power, to achieve, to create, to develop, to look and be the best we can. All are born motivations or wills derived from the will to love. We want to improve our homes, improve our work, etc., because we love ourselves.

The will to love is man's deep source of motivation and positive energy; it is the will that causes one to act firstly to survive, evolve, be accepted and achieve in life. At the very heart it is saying yes to life and realising that this is the case. What can create more positive energy than saying 'yes' to life and the acceptance of life?

Ask yourself, why do you get out of bed in the morning? You could just stay there and eventually fade away and die. It is because you love yourself you choose to survive? Why eat and drink? Why dress? Why go to work? Why socialise? Why achieve in life?

All actions are either done out of the will to love or the will not to love. The will to love is to take action, and to be able to love there has to be a clearly defined action or feeling. The will to love is the reason you do get out of bed everyday, you choose life for yourself.

Feelings = Action / Action = Feelings

The will to love in this day and age is what Nietzsche describes in Thus Spoke Zararthustra in the setting of goals to improve oneself to become one's highest hope – for here the will to love when realized really does enable you to become all you can be – The Super You.

Over indulgence in self-love in life results in greed and a will to power that then creates or becomes misaligned, misdirected and through negative energy immoral and evil, for the will to love or power becomes egotistical and the foundations of morality are forgotten for the sake of the self. Complete selfishness in a willingness not to share in your success or share the love is the dysfunctional behaviour of an individual in spiritual decline.

The will to love is the motivation that drives you to live the lifestyle you choose or would most desire. They say that money is the root of all evil but all money is a vehicle for you to live the lifestyle you would choose. In M. Scott Peck's 'The Road Less Travelled' he diagnoses real love as the ability to nurture someone else's spiritual growth, and the opposite force to love is not hate but laziness. What is your own definition of Love?

There are 8 simple components of the will to love, which could be broken down into so many more areas such as emotions, feelings....

Choice of Love

To love = Taking action to love (T)
Or
To not Love = No action to love or laziness (N)

Action of Love

Giving Love = Giving love through action or not giving love through no action / laziness (G)
Or
Receiving Love = Choosing to receive love through another's action or not receive love (R)

Direction of Love

Subjective Love = Self Love (S)
Or
Objective Love = Love of another person or object (O)

Type of Love

Unconditional Love = Love without condition / To love more or as
    much as the self (U)
Or
Conditional Love = Love with condition / To love less than the self (C)

Each action can be explained. For example, when a mother cuddles her
new born baby, the love can be defined as TGOU. The choice to love, the
action giving love; the direction is objective and it is unconditional love.

Another example in a relationship where an individual does not love the
other would be NROC. The choice not to love, the choice to receive, love
of the self and conditional.

In any relationship the equilibrium, or love utopia, is loving another
person as much as you love yourself. The ideal is unconditional love.

So many relationships fail because of conditions and the expectations
of being loved before giving love. Unfortunately this becomes the case
for so many people because when they have given unconditionally they
may have been let down either in childhood or their early relationships.
Hence the application of conditions and the expectation of being loved
or receiving love first.

A person's expectations of a relationship and love determine the
relationship.

Some relationships become business contracts that are negotiated on the
basis of what I get out of you and what you get from me.

Where is the love?

> *M. Scott Peck defines love -"I define love thus: The will to extend
> one's self for the purpose of nurturing one's own or another's spiritual
> growth."*

> *At the outset I would like to comment briefly on this definition before
> proceeding to a more thorough elaboration. First, it may be noticed*

that it is a teleological definition; the behaviour is defined in terms of the goal or purpose it seems to serve – in this case, spiritual growth.

….Second, it may be noticed that, as defined, love is a strangely circular process. For the process of extending one's self is an evolutionary process. When one has successfully extended one's limits, one has then grown into a lager state of being. Thus the act of loving is an act of self-evolution even when the purpose of the act is someone else's growth. It is through reaching toward evolution that we evolve.

….Third this unitary definition of love includes self-love with love for the other. Since I am human and you are human, to love humans means to love myself as well as you. To be dedicated to human spiritual development is to be dedicated to the race of which we are apart, and this therefore means dedication to our own development as well as 'theirs'. Indeed, as has been pointed out, we are incapable of loving another unless we love ourselves, just as we are incapable of teaching our children self discipline unless we ourselves are self disciplined. It is actually impossible to forsake our own spiritual development in favour of someone else's. We cannot forsake self-discipline and at the same time be disciplined in our care for another. We can not be a source of strength unless we nurture our own strength. As we proceeded in our exploration of the nature of love, I believe it will become clear that not only do self love and love of others go hand in hand but that ultimately they are indistinguishable.

Fourth, the act of extending one's limits implies effort. One extends one's limits only by exceeding them, and exceeding limits requires effort. When we love someone our love becomes demonstrable or real only through our exhertion – through the fact that for that someone (or for oneself) we take an extra step or walk an extra mile. Love is not effortless. To the contrary, love is effortful.

Finally, by the use of the word 'will' I have attempted to transcend the distinction between desire and action. Desire is not necessarily translated into action. Will is desire of sufficient intensity that is translated into action. The difference between the two is equal to the difference between saying 'I would like to go swimming tonight' and 'I will go swimming tonight'. Everyone in our culture desires to some extent to be loving, yet many are not in fact loving. I therefore conclude that the desire to love is not itself love. Love is as love does. Love is an act of will – namely, both an intention and an action.

Will also implies choice. We do not have to love. We choose to love. No matter how much we may think we are loving, if we are in fact not loving, it is because we have chosen not to love and therefore do not love despite our good intentions. On the other hand, whenever we do actually exert ourselves in the cause of spiritual growth, it is because we have chosen to do so. The choice to love has been made.
- M.Scott Peck – The Road Less Travelled

Therefore love is an act of will and will is an act of love.

Nietzsche says the source of man's strength or his motivation comes from the Will to Power, which is the will to overcome and improve our self. Therefore it is the will to become, which is driven by the will to love (self love). The opposite of this is the will to nothing, which means that we do not act or create or drive our self to act through laziness.

How many times have you told yourself off because you could not be bothered going for that run, washing the car, or going to the gym? Can you imagine what we could create if it were it not for pure bone idleness?

Now Nietzsche's next natural step was the Superman:

'Man is a rope, fastened between animal and superman – a rope over an abyss. A dangerous going across, a dangerous wayfaring, a dangerous looking back, a dangerous shuddering and staying still.'

'It is time for man to fix his goal. It is time for man to plant the seed of his highest hope.'

The Superman was misinterpreted with the pure Aryan of Hitler's mythology and it was this demonification that gave Nietzsche a notorious name. However based on the fact that within each era man is capable of maximum achievements, values and grandeur it is the Superman who lives life to the full ad infinitum. It is the striving to become a better person and to become all we can be. Based on the concept that there was no God and no afterlife then true motivation is to make the most of this life and everyday. In fact we should live our life like every day were to be our last.

What would you do if you were going to die and it was your last day? Make a full list.

What is stopping you from doing those things today?

In being able to become our own highest hope it is essential that we can move with change and not carry emotional baggage and pre-conditioning along with us that will hold us back. Let's focus on a model of change called the Change Transition Cycle. Transition psychology originated from work on death and grieving, family crisis and depression through the works of Parkes, Hill, Holmes and Rahe, and Kubler Ross, amongst other psychologists. The US Peace Corps introduced the model to volunteers in how to deal with dramatic change as part of their culture shock. It was then developed and adapted by Hopson into for career education and later to fit with theories of organizational change. Let's focus on people and the changes we go through in life and the choices we make in deciding how we react to change.

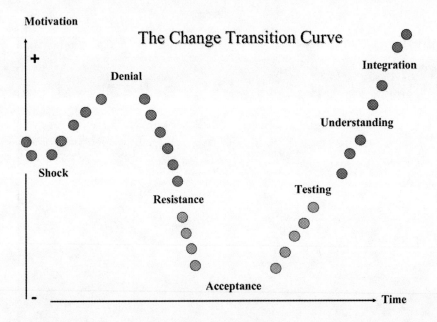

The process of adjusting to change has both a psychological and emotional impact as shown in the Transition Curve through the level of motivation and period of time from learning about the change.

There are three separate stages: Holding On, Letting Go and Moving On.

Holding On

Shock

With shock, if you have ever found yourself in this condition through the loss of a loved one, the breaking up of a relationship you valued, a car crash, etc., it is the literal feeling of not being able to function, to find ourself in another place when going through the motions, to be disturbed and overwhelmed. It can be the case where we find it hard or unable to reason and understand what is happening. When in this stage we find ourselves unable to make plans and take action because our behaviour is paralysed. People suffer with shock in different ways dependent upon the event and it is possible for an individual to suffer shock whilst another does not from the same event.

Denial

The denial stage is the belief that there is still something to cling on to, it is not over, or it is not going to happen. Here the belief has not changed and there will be a withdrawn process of denial. We see the news or change as trivial and often do not believe that a change is going to take place. This is a time where we retreat from reality to challenge our own beliefs and sum up the inner strength to cope with the situation.

Resistance

With the resistance stage it is the recognition that impending change is coming and we reactively resist the change. A different range of emotions can be experienced where the we fight with feelings of anger, resentment, jealousy, envy, hopelessness, powerlessness, possessiveness, obsessive behaviour, being fixated in the past, and can lead to depression and isolation. During this stage, we may try to hold on to the 'good old days'. People who live a reactive life continue to live in the first 3 stages and hold on to emotional baggage. This is negative energy.

Letting Go

Acceptance

Acceptance is the beginning of letting go of the resistance to the change, it is being able to accept and deal with the reality of the situation. Here we might not agree with the change itself but it is the realization that change will happen no matter what. For those holding on to emotional baggage or negative emotions it is the letting go of negative energy - it is freeing ourselves from bondage to the past or fear of the emerging future.

Testing

Once accepting the change we start to test the boundaries, moving out of our comfort zone. Dependent upon the success of the testing stage then depends upon the speed of transition we move with the change. Generally a real acceptance starts to happen because we have already started to move in a positive direction. It is essential to provide great praise and encouragement to oneself or another in this stage.

Moving On

Understanding

This stage is where we really understand why the change has happened by seeing the bigger picture. We will find benefits within the change and start to seek meaning as to why the change happened. Here the philosophical 'everything happens for a reason' type of statements become more matter of fact.

Integration

The final stage is the integration of the change in to our lives and with no holding on to negative emotions we are able to move forward with a positive vitality. This is business as usual and we are ready for a new and exciting challenge.

We all experience these stages after a change: however we will all move at different speeds through the transition hence how two people can experience the same change but be affected in different ways.

Now if we go back to the first three stages of the transition, 'Holding on', most people in life when changes occur continue to hold on and struggle to move to the acceptance stage. We can become resentful, uncomfortable or even lost. Psychologically this may lead to feelings of guilt, bitterness, anger, jealousy, frustration, remorse, etc., which are all negative emotions. This leads to blaming life, to *'it's not fair'*, or *'it's cruel world'*, or *'there's no such thing as God'*, to being a victim of life resulting from an unwillingness to move with change. There is also a kind of negative acceptance that we cannot move with the change. Rather than resisting at times, the feeling is one of giving up or the giving up of hope and, for some of us, the condemnation of life and the world. Our own subterranean map of the world suggests the world is a bad place, that life is hard, it's a cruel world, which is negative self conditioning through negative self talk.

What drives people's behaviour is what they think or feel. It is within the resistance stage that so many people live and remain. They carry baggage from past experiences and reactively carry negative energy around with them. Weighing them down, making the heart heavy, this is wasted energy that leads to psychosomatic illnesses caused by the mind. People who are reactive in life live in the resistance stage of holding on - as they cannot let go. How much negative energy do you carry around with you? An example of this destructive energy was a friend of mine's dad had a disagreement with the next door neighbour over a set of ladders over twenty years ago. When mentioned recently, the Father was bitter and angry at the neighbour, even though the event happened twenty years ago and the neighbour had moved on. Wasted energy. He was holding on to that negative energy all that time. I am sure you can recount your own stories of holding on and other people's. We need to let go of the negative energy, and through love forget and let go by accepting life; and then moving on.

How many of us go to work and act nicely to people all day yet when we get home we act reactively to the kids or to our spouse or partner, shouting and screaming without thinking, or kicking the dog or the cat? At the smallest of things? How come we can be so nice to people in work when stressed and then we reactively take it out on our loved ones for no good reason. They say you hurt the people you love the most but why should we? We should be choosing our own reaction and being extra nice to the people we love. What about negative energy around friends or family we perhaps have fallen out with, and therefore not been able to forgive the past. How can we fall out with our own daughter to the point that we would never want to see her again and then hold on to those negative emotions for the rest of our life - move on - don't take those emotions to the grave or let them take you there.

Negative Energy

So how does that link to the Change Transition? There are so many people in this world who have gone over to the Dark Side of the Force! If you take a look at the diagram below you will notice the Danger Zone, which represents the trap of the Dark Side. Here we do not accept the changes in life; there is an immense amount of Negative Energy e.g. bitterness, resentment and anger that is wasted energy. I have known people hold on to negative feelings for years, which hold them back. This Negative Energy is energy that could be used for a better purpose. And all the time we hold on to the negative feelings the more they will make you physically ill, in this case psychosomatic illness - illness created by your mind. We live in a reactive world where everything else is to blame, other people, the tools, and the world. Anything except our self is to blame or the complete opposite we completely blame the self. People who live in a reactive world are bitter, jealous, envious, resentful, and angry etc they hold on to negative energy and it is killing them. It is the source of all stress. There will also be a lack of self-love.

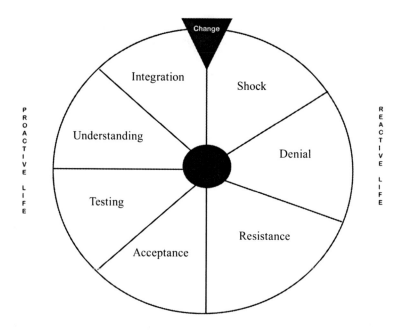

Positive Energy	Negative Energy
A proactive person	A reactive person
Moving with change	Reacting to change
Consciously choosing your own response	Holding on to negative emotions
Accepting life	Holding on to negative feelings
Saying Yes to life	Blaming life
Changing what you can	Not being able to change
Positive outlook - Optimist	Negative outlook - Pessimist
Living the dream	Living the nightmare

There are three key factors if you are to truly maximise the will to love when moving through changes in life with positive energy.

1. We have the freedom to choose our own response to any given situation.

2. We have to take action and move out of our comfort zone (Homeostasis).

3. We need to direct the source of our motivation to consistently maintain the momentum.

Every experience in our life shapes the person we are and if we react positively to both the good and the bad we will spiritually grow.

So we have established our true motivation, the will to love and that we truly want to become all that we can be. Next we move onto Nietzsche's Eternal Recurrence, which is a state of mind as opposed to the enlightenment and categorization of the universe. Nietzsche says that history moves in cycles and that everything that was comes around time and time again. This is a moral theory as opposed to a theory of the cosmos. Quite simply, perhaps there has been a special moment in your life that you would be willing to live your whole life again to relive that moment or moments, and therefore you are willing to live your life over and over again. In fact on a larger scale our actions and intentions should have such generosity and grandeur that we should be able and willing to repeat them over again for infinity. It is to embrace life unconditionally by saying yes to life.

> *'My formula for the greatness of a human being is amor fati: That only wants to be different – not forward, not backwards, not in all eternity. Not merely bear what is necessary, still less conceal it…but love it.'*

We take the good with the bad because we relish all aspects of life. Life is a spiritual journey of self-development and self-becoming. If we can say yes to life then all our negative emotions can be replaced by a completely positive outlook, feelings and energy.

> *Nietzsche's Amor Fati – 'This joy is the formula for the greatness of the human being. It is to live with passion.'*

It is finding that passion in our life and living with passion.

Finally Nietzsche's aesthetic view on life was that each life was a tragedy and truly what man is capable of understanding and creating comes from within oneself. Unquestionably the power in one life is enough to create a thousand worlds. Each life is a tale in the making – it is an epic. Life is a gift – something to be thankful for and to celebrate everyday.

Nietzsche's life affirming view gives us a positive state of mind and therefore a positive attitude. We can build upon a solid foundation based on our state of mind and the choices we make in life aiming to become our highest hope –the Super You.

In life, attitude breeds attitude and behaviour breeds behaviour. We attract people, situations and events in line with our dominant thoughts into our life. Positive thoughts and actions will make positive things happen. Our thoughts shape our life and most illnesses are psychosomatic illnesses brought on by negative thoughts and emotions linked to holding on within the danger zone of the change transition.

This means we have a choice in life to shape our own fate. We could choose to be negative, pessimistic and bitter about life but where will that get us? Yes it is hard to be positive and optimistic all of the time but we have the opportunity to shape our own character by shaping our thoughts and realising our feelings. It is character building that makes the difference, not small changes to our personality or behaviour. We can't act like we love life if we don't really believe it in our subconscious. Well we could, but deep down our feelings within our subconscious would produce the final outcome.

Right now we are interested in self-conditioning and saying Yes to life, and Yes to our self. It is truly defining our attitude towards life and our self that makes the difference between being a winner or a loser. What we think about our self, which is our self-concept, and what we feel about our self, which is our self-esteem need to be on parallel. It is how we feel which determines our inner character and therefore it will determine our self-concept. The critical determining factor is that how we really feel will shape our self-talk this affects our self-image and hence our actions reinforce your feelings and beliefs. For example, we might be able to hide behind a masked personality in pretending our self-concept is high e.g. being arrogant but hiding insecurities with feelings of inferiority. These feelings shape our self-image, which then overcompensates to hide the insecurity or confirms the self-complex. It is our subconscious feelings and associations that will determine our actions. It is important to take time to really think what we would like our self to be and then shape our self-ideal. Working from our self-ideal we should then shape our self-concept and esteem. By then generating the ideal feelings and actively changing our physiology we can make deep subconscious changes that we can embed through reinforced behaviour and belief.

Example: Shows the negative spiral of low self-esteem, which affects the self concept leading to negative self-talk and the lowering of expectations of the ideal self.

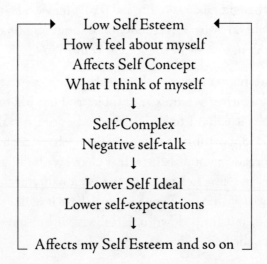

What is your Self-Esteem? (What you really feel about yourself)

What is your Self Concept? (What you think of yourself)

What is your Self-Ideal? (What you would like to be like)

If we let our self-esteem lead, which is how we feel at the time then generally, when in situations we don't like or find challenging our negative self talk will take over. What needs to happen for us to take control is to lead from our self-ideal and generate the feelings of that ideal to positively affect our self-esteem.

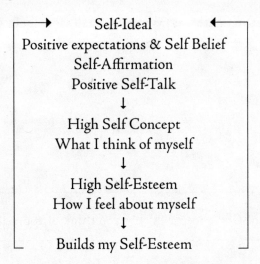

Self-Ideal
Positive expectations & Self Belief
Self-Affirmation
Positive Self-Talk
↓
High Self Concept
What I think of myself
↓
High Self-Esteem
How I feel about myself
↓
Builds my Self-Esteem

What we need on a feeling level is a definite Yes to life and our self. This with a passion and belief in whom we are, what we are trying to achieve and where we want to go opens up the sky to a sun shining with glorious possibilities and opportunities.

This means that you have a choice in life to be all that we are; you alone can decide to be positive or negative. By being positive and having a positive attitude it gives us the right frame of mind to shape our own future. However being positive is not enough in itself; to make positive changes in our life we need to act upon our feelings. The elegance and simplicity of the positive mind provides a kind of autogenic conditioning that gives us the inspiration to make dramatic structural changes in our life. By saying Yes to life we are also saying yes to our self. In fact we should re-affirm everyday acceptance of the self by repeating in a mirror 'I like/love myself'. Positive affirmations help to create the reality for the mind.

Affirmations are best used first thing in the morning or last thing at night when we are in our alpha state of consciousness, which means we still have access to the subconscious. Our affirmations need to be positive, specific, personal and in the present tense. We need to write down our affirmations and repeat them daily taking full accountability.

Linking back to Festinger's theory of Cognitive Dissonance, once we have decided on a belief, then the mind will supply the relevant information to support that belief. Liking our self and believing in our self are the healthiest things we can do in life because if we have self-belief and we like our self then our self-esteem will be high, self-esteem being what we really feel about our self, and so this will generate good thoughts, resulting in a high self-concept – what we think about our self. It is the belief that generates high self-esteem because we really do like our self or really do believe we are a likeable person or we really do believe we are good at a particular skill. It is this acceptance of life and acceptance of the self, this saying yes to life as a tale in the making, and re-enforcing these feelings with a passion and belief that will help us to become a better person.

It gives us the platform to become our highest hope and shape our own future through choice.

Remember you are accountable and definitely in control of your life as an interdependent individual within the species of the Earth.

Exercise: Under the specific headings below write down ways to help you develop, through direction, realisation and discipline.

Self Development = What will you do to develop yourself?
Self Direction = How will you give yourself direction?
Self Realisation = How will you realize your potential?
Self Discipline = How will you maintain discipline?

Self Development	Self Direction
Self Realisation	Self Discipline

It is our expectations in life that will become our realities and, through the will to love, it will enable us to act in a positive way to set the right causes in motion to get the right effects; it is understanding our inner goals, targets, and dreams because the hearts content is different for everyone. Some say that all human action is motivated by dissatisfaction, but surely if it were dissatisfaction, that would not create the right feeling to be consistently motivated and only limited or small changes could take place before returning back to the norm. It is the people who, through dissatisfaction, conjure up a powerful vision of the goal that make long-term consistent changes. Once again it is about creating the right feeling. If every life is a tale in the making (and it is) then I would sooner be motivated by the dream and all the wonderful feelings it creates. Where would gratification for the present moment lie? Dreams are all about spiritual growth and continually re-inventing yourself to become all you are.

'That which does not kill me makes me stronger' - Nietzsche

Motivated by the Will to love which is the Will to act.

Nietzsche Scenario

Imagine you are like Fredriech Nietzsche. You are working upon your latest masterpiece and decide to walk through the Swiss Alps of St.Moritz for inspiration. You take daily walks up to the highest peak to look out upon the vast array of mountain tops. In this moment how and what do you feel?

Were you at one with nature feeling the wind upon your face as you looked out upon a scene of infinite beauty? What did you feel? Happiness, sadness, or inspiration? Maybe its magnitude inspired you to say yes to life, yes to greatness, yes to the dream, and yes to the feeling of what is right in life.

If you get in touch with your feelings and dreams then you know what is right in life and what is right for you, and it is that holistic feeling of what is right that creates your own values system. If you can condition yourself to accept everything that is wonderful around you and feel at one with your inner values then you can create a beliefs system that, as an individual code of conduct, will enable you to achieve your aspired greatness.

> *'It's an energy field created by all living things, it surrounds us, it penetrates us, it binds the galaxy together' - Obi Wan describes the force in Star Wars.*

Your life does not have to be determined by what happens to you for it is the attitude you bring to life that will determine your future by choosing how you react to life. It is not what life brings you that shapes your future but what you choose to let affect your life and what you choose to change. A positive attitude and outlook in life is a catalyst, a splinter in the mind that starts the journey and allows you to realize the freedom of your own actions in living the life you choose to live.

> *You have the freedom to choose your reaction and your life – choose wisely and change your life with positive energy!*

Life Changing Questions

What is driving you?
How strong is your will?
How much do you love yourself?
How much do you love other people / other things?
What part of the change transition do you tend to live in?
Are you a reactive or proactive person?

When are you reactive?

What negative energy do you carry with you?

How can you change it into positive energy?

What is your life's tale?

What is your attitude?

Do you say yes to life? Yes to yourself?

What do you choose?

> "Man alone of all beings when addressed by the voice of Being, experiences the marvel of marvels: That what is - is." - Martin Heidegger

> 'Realize my child that you are shaped by every experience from birth, sculpted and layered to become a slave to your conditioning, reactive in response and thought, bound to circumstances, fallen from grace. Now open yourself to the ultimate power the 'will to love' and enlighten yourself in knowing all action is persistence of that will to love oneself! Awaken to your own brilliance and become a bringer of light to the people. Surround yourself with positive energy and be free of the shackles, be free of the dark night, and see for the first time.'
>
> Twilight falls, lightning strikes, end to nothing, beginning with all.
>
> 'Where is your talent? What do you do? What do you give? What do you love? Where do you create? When do you shine you crazy diamond?'

Summary

1. The driving force in life is the will to love; every positive action we make is generated by the will to love.

2. The opposite of the will to love is the will to nothing (Procrastination / Laziness)

3. Nietzsche's Superman was a vision of the Better-man always striving to develop and spiritually grow to become all we can be - our highest hope.

4. That we should say Yes to life and to ourselves and embrace life as a gift

5. Each life is a tale in the making – it is an epic

6. Attitude breeds attitude

7. Your beliefs create your realities

8. The ideal is unconditional love of the self and of others

9. Choose to change your life with positive energy

    "Our lives are not determined by what happens to us but by how we react to what happens, not by what life brings to us, but by the attitude we bring to life. A positive attitude causes a chain reaction of positive thoughts, events, and outcomes. It is a catalyst, a spark that creates extraordinary results. - Anon

Chapter 6: The Super You

"You are only coming through in waves,
Your lips move but I can't hear what you're saying,
When I was a child I caught a fleeting glimpse
Out of the corner of my eye,
I turned to look but it was gone
I cannot put my finger on it
The child has grown, the dream has gone.
I have become comfortably numb."
Pink Floyd - Comfortably Numb

So we have a destiny to fulfil, an inner calling and a sense of purpose in this life. We understand the will to love is the driving force and ultimate motivation guiding us to become all we can be, our highest hope – the Super You. Also that our life is a tale in the making of epic proportions and accepting life by saying yes to life will create positive energy and a positive outcome which will fill our life with abundance through the will to love.

To be able to realize the Super You we need to have self-awareness of who we really are, what we believe and what we want.

Who are you?

Now we have said Yes to life but who are you? Who am I? Who are we all?

Saying Yes to life is saying yes we choose to become all that we can be and that with a positive mindset using the will to love (to act) we will move forward firmly towards our goal - the ideal or super self.

However you need to know one very important thing – you need to know thyself and say yes to thyself! Here we are confronted with the issue of identity. If we have a solid identity then the foundations are there to build upon. If we start with shaky foundations or an unknown or mixed identity then it is hard to maintain the achievement of the goal consistently. For we live in a grey twilight of uncertainty, mixed emotions and lack of direction.

Who are we? Why are we here? What purpose or meaning do we have for our existence? Who do we associate with? What are our values? Our beliefs? How do others see us? What conflicting beliefs do we have?

It is time to explore your very self to evaluate who you really are. Start by answering the questions above to start to associate with your own psychological make up. What is your identity? What do you identify with?

Our identity is made up of lots of different components ranging from a number of considerations i.e.

Your name? Your age?
Your gender? When and where you were born?
Ethnic background?
Where you live?
Your parents' values?
Your family / friends' values?
Your own principles and values?
Who you associate with?
What you want from life?
Why you are here?
The meaning to your life?

Your inner most beliefs?

Your most common traits? Your personality?

What you look like?

Who you want to be like?

Our identity is influenced through biological, psychological and social structures such as our sex/gender, our personality, our parents, our schooling, our friends, our opportunities in life.

In attempting to realize or find the Super You it is important to have a solid sense of identity. On this basis we also need to establish which of our values may contradict one another so that there is no block in energy or identity, e.g. being married and having numerous affairs could be an example of two completely different values, which are bound to pull us apart resulting in negative energy being directed in towards the body instead of out in to the world. (Although that will also generate a lot of negative energy out in the world in other people's lives.)

Why are you here?

Let's go back to the Magician's question at the start of the book – why are you here?

Continue to ask why to every answer, answering as honestly as you can.

Man will always attempt and strive to be like his God, as God is the most perfect example of 'being' that could exist. So aspirationally we want to be like God – it is a subconscious calling. However we will always fail because of man made morality that is echoed by human dualism. Let's say God has no opposite or no dualistic tendencies because God is beyond good and evil, right and wrong. God is beyond Mankind's categorization or definition and we live in a dualistic world of self made concepts and choices.

Ask yourself what you believe: Is there a God? Do you follow a religion? Your own religion? Do you believe in the Teleological Argument that the universe has a set design and purpose? Or the Cosmological Argument with the universe being here at all, it must mean something has created it as it can not surely have come from nothing? Or the Ontological Argument which is simply from the examination of the concept of God that the God from the concept must exist? Or do you think it is all chaos? Or do you have your own argument? Write down your own beliefs now because it is important to have an understanding to have a strong sense of identity. What do you believe?

Here we start with a re-evaluation of all your beliefs, values and law tables.

What is your deep inner reason for being here?
What will you choose?

The Kingdom of Camelot

King Arthur was caught within a dream, awoken by a spirit beckoning him to the woods beyond Camelot. In the middle of the night he rode out of Camelot into the fields with a fresh breeze upon his face eager in anticipation but gaunt with fear. Deep into the forest he rode as if deep into his own heart till at last there beside the lake lay Lancelot and Queen Guinevere, his most trusted friend and wife in betrayal. Arthur in his pain rode back to Camelot with a choice to make – would he forgive his wife such treachery at the expense of the Kingdom and leave Camelot or would he banish her for the sake of the ideal of the Kingdom of Camelot? What would you choose?

Although Arthur loved Guinevere dearly he chose what he felt was the greater good, maintaining the Kingdom of Camelot. He sacrificed his love and was driven to banish Guinevere to live the remainder of her life within the church, punishing her for her treachery. It was not until the end of his days that he returned to Guinevere and gave her his forgiveness and gallantly asked for his. Life is full of choices that shape you to become all that you can be. Most choices do not carry as much dilemma as the scenario discussed but life will continually throw at you the roads of contradiction.

In a dualistic world you cannot go left if you choose to go right – but life does offer you the choice to decide your own fate.

The freedom to choose?

Starting with the choices about you…as life is all about choices.

'I wish the ring had never come to me, I wish none of this had ever happened,' said Frodo.

'So do all who live to see such times, but that is not for them to decide. All we have to decide is what to do with the time given to us,' replies Gandalf. – A scene from The Lord of the Rings

What decisions would you make and how would you respond to each of the following situations?

In work you have been producing quality material and outputs but have been getting little recognition, what do you do?

Your partner has been unfaithful what do you do?

A friend has been talking about you behind your back?

You're mugged in a big city?

If you were reactive in all of these situations you would blame other people, it's work's fault, it's my partner's, or even worse, her lover's fault, that friend is an evil let down and all people from big cities are a shower of muggers. (Which is not true may I add!!). This is all based on assumptions, which is then based on your own individual map of the world. This map is shaped by your beliefs of the world and when certain things happen you react. In fact you react so badly sometimes you can expend negative energy for years, as discussed earlier through the change transition. (For some people, a lifetime).

So here is the moral cleansing part, which is a baptism of fire, instead of turning to the **'Dark Side'** we need to be proactive. In each of the situations we start with our self and realize that we have the freedom to choose our own reaction to any given situation. Next we look at the part we have played in the situation for example if we had neglected our partner then maybe that has led to their unfaithfulness. We should always look at our self first before projecting our energy outwards, it is the 'think' before we act or before we speak. Then we make decisions based on clear objective thought that will not hold us back in the future. It is also facing the day with a clean slate instead of emotional hang-ups through choosing our state of mind for the day.

In Covey's The Seven Habits of Highly Effective People, Covey talks about Victor Frankl and the last ultimate freedom, which is the freedom to choose our own response from any given stimulus. Now positive and proactive thinking are excellent ways to develop a positive outcome but it is actually the action or response that creates our own fate.

We have become so reactive in life that we forget that we do have choices and that we are free to make them. We can choose our response to any given situation - no matter what; choosing that response in every situation is the hard part because we need to be living in a state of positive control and action.

We choose our identity, our beliefs, values, friends and the person we want to be. We can also choose our own goals and way of life, the hard part is taking consistent action.

Why the easiest choice?

What do we mean by the easiest choice? In this context the easiest choice is the one that amounts to the least work and maintains the status quo. Why then do so many people give up on the dream or their ultimate goals?

Is it because of laziness or lack of desire to achieve the goal?

It can be for a number of reasons:-

> They lack the belief that it is possible.
> They fear the hard work they would have to put in to achieve the goal.
> The desire is not great enough.
> They are too scared to act through fear.
> They prefer the easiest choice - laziness.
> They fear failure.
> *They fear success.*

So why then do people make the easiest choice most of the time? Quite simply we are creatures who like to stay within our comfort zone (we become literally comfortably numb) and we are not willing to put the effort in to change. Also, to make that change, we normally have to stand out and be different which can sometimes go against the social norm. The longing to belong becomes more important and hence we conform to others' standards and expectations.

> *This "homeostatic impulse" is another term for your comfort zone. It is your unconscious tendency to be drawn irresistibly toward what you have always done. This inability to break free of the tentacles of the past is the reason most people accomplish far less than they are capable of and remain unfulfilled and dissatisfied for most of their lives. - Brian Tracy – Maximum Achievement*

Tracy goes on to explain that this mechanism maintains balance within the body and that when stretched our natural instinct is to go back to our comfort zone or to build a new one. Tracy also talks of a term called 'Psychosclerosis' which means hardening of the attitudes or a hardening of our beliefs or beliefs system. The opposite of this is flexibility.

The hardening of the attitudes is the way in which we form habits, which are then monitored by our homeostatic mechanism. It is essential to monitor and understand our habits because they become our character and our character becomes our destiny.

The Iceberg Analogy in the forming of habits

> *Into the hands of every individual is given a marvelous power for good or evil – the silent, unconscious, unseen influence of his life. This is simply the constant radiation of what man really is, not what he pretends to be. - William George Jordan*

The iceberg represents on the surface the conscious mind, which is an eighth of the mind. What is visible on the surface from an observer's point of view is the person's behaviour – the objective experience viewed by another. Below the surface are the other seven eighths of the subconscious mind, which from an observer's point of view cannot be seen. What drives a person's behaviour underneath the surface is their feelings and thoughts – the subjective experience known to the self.

This is where as humans we control our instinctual impulses because even though we may be thinking or feeling one thing we can act or behave in a totally different manner. However the majority of the time we do act in line with our thoughts and feelings and they are driven by our beliefs and values deeply embedded within our subconscious. We form habits that are consistent with our map or beliefs of the world and everyone has their own individual map of the world, which, as discussed earlier, has been designed in the forming of our identity.

It is important to understand our identity's make-up to understand what our habits are.

Some habits go deeper than others because the motivation is greater due to a certain belief or value the habit is based upon.

> *For our purposes, we will define a habit as the intersection of knowledge, skill and desire. Knowledge is the theoretical paradigm, the what to do and why. Skill is the how to do. And desire is the motivation, the want to do. In order to make something a habit in our lives, we have to have all three. - Stephen R Covey*

If we attempt purely to change our behaviour without changing the way we feel or our beliefs then the change in habit will not last long. On this basis we can choose our own habits through choosing or changing our beliefs about the world. In breaking a habit it normally means stepping out of the comfort zone and a certain amount of hard work, which then takes us back to the easiest choice.

Less work makes hard work seem like the hard choice when it is just as easy a choice to make....we need to focus on the benefits of changing the habit and the consequences of not. If the benefits far outweigh the consequences then the pleasure is far greater than the pain, so change. However if we choose to dwell on making the change then once again we are expending negative energy by stagnating in our comfort zone.

So we have to be stretched...

> *Fear causes hesitation and hesitation will cause your worst fears to come true. Bodicifer – Point Break*

There is no such thing as failure. There is consistent action in line with our beliefs. And if in our mind we think we have failed remind yourself we have not. We are acting in line with our beliefs.

What more can we ask for in life than a man or woman willing to live, act and die by their values and beliefs. It is the ability to keep trying when we do not get the desired results.

Who do you talk to every time before making a decision?

Our self

How many times have you said 'I'm of two minds'? Generally we are faced with the roads of contradiction mentioned earlier. Here are some of those roads or choices - which ones would you make?

You are in love with two people; one has been a close friend for years and the other lives in Italy, somewhere you have always wanted to live. Who do you choose?

You have the choice between continuing to work for the company you have been with for 20 years with a lot of security or starting your own business which could make you a lot of money but be less predictable. What action do you take?

You play for the team you have supported since a boy but now have the chance to play for a team who can meet your aspirations. They are both in the same league. Which do you choose?

Your career is taking off but it means more travel with the new promotion and this means seeing less of your family. What do you choose?

Lastly you stand before God at the gate of heaven and he says you need to pick the chicken or the egg and only one choice will get you into heaven! Which do you choose?

Ok what's the point? (Not with the chicken and the egg but which one did come first? I'm sure God knows if you believe in God – perhaps it was both! At the end of the day you choose and live by the choice you make, you are shaped by that choice because if the egg never got you in to heaven your conditioning might be that eggs are really bad things in the future!). The point here illustrates the choices upon the roads of contradiction that you have faced during your life. Sometimes when you go through one door the other closes and you are destined upon a path going right as opposed to left. Sometimes those paths will entwine. Also when one door closes another one opens.

When faced with these choices the one person we will definitely discuss and mull it over with will be our self.

If you were sat in a quiet room with no distractions and decided we were not going to think of anything or talk to anyone (even though there is no-one there) just how much thinking and talking will we do? Because the person we will be talking to is our self. Our self-talk is so vitally important because it is linked to our self-ideal, concept and esteem.

The voices in our head question our ability to perform any given task and establish the desire or motivation to complete the task and then we decide.

" You know I need to get up for that jog *but hey I could go tomorrow* but I need to get fit, *yeah but I'm not in so bad shape.* Yes you're right but I want to go running to get some fresh air and I will be focused for the day. *But we haven't had that much sleep and we will be tired for work and this bed is really warm. Hmmm, let's have 5 more minutes…*"

How many times have you had conversations like that in your head before making a decision?

In fact the voices in our head tend either to be critical and doubting or self affirming - which one do you listen to the most?

What is the one question we should ask our self in any situation?

The one question is: 'What would the Super You do in this situation?'

And if you answer the question truthfully then you will always have an answer in line with what you always want to be.

In fact when the negative, self doubting, critical voice takes over in our head we should ask our self what would the Super You do in this situation and act accordingly.

Why do we have limitations and boundaries on what we can achieve?

The Logical and Creative Brain

Researchers Roger Sperry and Robert Ornstein from the University of California discovered that the two halves of the human brain work in different ways. This research had taken 25 years and won them the Nobel Prize for medicine. Their work led to understanding the two hemispheres of the neo-cortex of the brain and that these two halves had two different functions and characteristics.

Although they work in different ways, they can work together or separately, contributing and combining each other's faculties or working against each other. In most people one hemisphere dominates the other. The left-brain deals with verbal ideas and uses words to describe things. Its characteristics are logic, lists, words, numbers, sequences, facts, reasoning, it thinks linearly and analyses by breaking things down into digestible chunks.

The right side of the brain relates to gestures or pictures, it synthesizes by putting parts together to make the whole. The right side's characteristics are colour, imagination, daydreaming, intuition, rhythm and music, instinct, and it thinks holistically by seeing patterns and ideas linked to the whole.

So the brain can simply be broken down into two halves, which makes you at times the two people you are; the left logical side and the right creative side. The characteristics of the left side of the brain are reasoning and realism with the right being imagination and creativity. This natural dualism means that the left-sided brain will think limitations while the right-sided brain thinks it can achieve anything. The left-side of the brain is very logical in that one idea follows another whilst the right-side thinks holistically, creating ideas through patterns to make the whole.

The left is interested in the detail - the right the big picture.

Left Brain and Right Brain Comparison of Characteristics

Left Brain Mode	Right Brain Mode
Verbal Using words to name, define, describe	Non-Verbal Awareness of things but minimal connection with words
Analytical Figuring things out step by step and part by part	Synthetic Putting things together to form wholes
Concrete Relating things that are at the present moment	Symbolic Using a symbol to stand for something e.g. "+" stands for addition
Analogical Seeing likeness between things: understanding of metamorphic relationships	Abstract Taking out of a small bit of information and using it to represent the whole thing
Temporal Keeping track of time, sequencing one thing after another. Doing first things first, second and so on.	Non-Temporal Without a sense of time
Rational Drawing conclusions based on reason and facts	Non-Rational Not requiring a basis of reason or facts: willingness to suspend judgement

Digital Using numbers as in counting	Spatial Seeing where things are in relation to other things and how parts go together to from a whole
Logical Drawing conclusions based on logic; one thing following another in logical order	Intuitive Making leaps of thoughts often based on incomplete patterns, hunches, feelings, or visual images
Linear Thinking in terms of linked ideas. One thought directly following another, often leading to a convergent conclusion.	Holistic Seeing whole things all at once: perceiving the overall patterns and structures, often leading to divergent conclusions.

(Table Taken from Catch the Bug Ltd©)

In Chapter 1 we discussed the concept that were two people, our conscious self and the subconscious greater self who acts as our inner guide through life.

Now this is where both sides of the brain tie into our personality and conscious and subconscious states. The logical side questions *'Is this right or wrong?' 'Is this good or evil?'* The left side thinks and thinks logically. It is the left side of your brain that questions and doubts what you can achieve based on what's real. Therefore this part of us tends to say *'I can't do that'* or *'It's impossible to do'* by setting limitations and can be the negative voice within.

The right side of our brain completely opposes this in the sense that it is naturally creative and designed to believe that anything is possible. The right-side of the brain does not see limitations, it's in a natural positive state and says that *'We can do this'* or *'I can do that.'*

The right side of the brain does not categorize an action into good or evil because it does not think; it feels whether a thing is right or wrong, good and evil. It is a special awareness, psyche or intuition that is linked more to the subterranean world of dreams and the sub-conscious. Our normal conscious mind naturally is more logical because we live in an ordered society, with law tables, categorizations, definitions, guidelines, morality.

Only until recently school education enforced the 3 Rs, riting, reading and rithmetic, which were tailored to the left side of the brain, mostly excluding the right-sided functions of the brain. Nowadays there is a lot more practical development in GCSEs and A levels than that of the old revise and be tested O and A levels.

The main point here is that we are a condition of society, upbringing, history, and we are conditioned to listen to the left side of the brain that says 'I can't'. We also listen to the left side because the right side is challenging us to put a lot of hard work into realising and achieving our dreams. Unfortunately the opposite of love is laziness and yes we are all lazy because there are times we take the easy way out. Some of us take this way out more than others. We also listen to the left side because of conformity; because at times, to achieve our dreams, we have to be different from other people. This frightens the status quo and we conform by not making the effort because of fear. We prefer to belong than stand out.

We live in a dualistic world of good and evil, right and wrong. This man made duality stretches back within all myths and religion. It would also seem to be dualistic on the basis of our conscience experience of the material world and the mental realm of thoughts and feelings. A large part of the duality in life within our way of thinking has been derived from Plato and Aristotle.

Plato (428 – 347BC) wrote many books that creatively included characters of his day such as Socrates. His books were lessons within stories. His main theory was the theory of eternal forms. He believed in eternal and immutable patterns, which were both spiritual and abstract in nature. Within the world of senses everything flows and then passes away. But there is another world, the world of ideas, which is eternal and perfect. For example the idea of the horse must exist for horses to exist. This is quite a creative and imaginative theory pointing to Plato being a right-sided thinker (potentially).

Then we have Aristotle (384 – 322BC) who was definitely very logical in his thinking. He classified the sciences in a very organized and logical way by suggesting that all forms have set characteristics. Therefore all things that exist can be categorized by their set characteristics; this points to Aristotle being very left-sided in his approach.

Plato's philosophy of the grand picture is the world of ideas leading to idealism where the only thing that really exists is the world of ideas. Aristotle, the materialist and protagonist of logic, believed that the only things we can know is the world itself.

The ideas of Plato and Aristotle are good examples that demonstrate not only how the way the world was shaped into a dualistic world but how undecided we have become upon the world around us through this duality. (Is it all idea or is it part of a material function? Is their spirit or soul bound to either belief about the world?) It is possible to fit Plato as right brained philosopher and Aristotle as left. The fact is they both had a good proportion of both, like each one of us, both trying to make sense of the world like each one of us. Showing a preference for how they approach the world either through the logical or the creative, helps to predict our outcomes. Plato the imaginative storyteller, and Aristotle the scientist and realist.

The left side of the brain will realize the consequences of any action and what the limits upon the individual will be. The right side brained people are not better than the left or vice versa because the left side will protect us at times and the right is prone to blowing things out of proportion in negative situations. It is having a combination of both sides that enable us to function effectively, having an awareness of how to maximize them both to our advantage.

We are born to win but conditioned to lose.

We are conditioned to disproportionately use the left more than the right and set limits on what we can achieve.

So how do we become right-brain activists? Can we all become Mozarts? No, perhaps not. The fact is if you listen and tap into the right side of the brain you can realize that anything is possible. If you listen to that second voice in your head you will realize how great you can become. How do we overcome our left sided tendencies then to achieve greatness? It's quite simple. We combine the left and right side and bring the brain together as one. Our Self-talk, based upon our chosen beliefs and values, convinces us to make effective decisions without the doubts and limitations.

This is part of the reason why multiple personalities, characters, masks and personas develop within man.

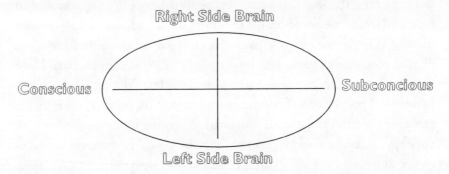

We have conversations with ourselves! How many times have you talked to yourself out loud, no matter inside your head? These conversations are diplomatic exchanges between the conscious and sub-conscious mind and the right and left side of the brain.

Who is the Super You?

It is a matter of having a true appreciation of the thought process behind our own self and finding out where our strengths and development areas lie. This, coupled with a clear focus on a positive attitude with positive language and beliefs, will help us find the Super You.

We start to think of what we would really like to achieve and then what do we feel? Exhilaration? Excitement? No, the left side says, *'Wait a minute what's realistic? Do you really think you can do that? It will take hard work. Time and effort. You will probably start and then what do we do 9 times out of 10? Give up.'*

A positive attitude needs to be coupled with positive actions and they have to be proactive actions. Our proactive actions need to be based on our beliefs, which will generate the feelings we need to make the changes. This, with an appreciation that anything is possible, gives us the opportunity to re-evaluate our life and re-program our own mind. By creating a whirlwind of positivity about life and listening to our true feelings we can create values and beliefs that develop character and proactivity.

Beliefs + Values = Thoughts/Feelings + Choice = Proactivity
Proactivity = Desired Behaviour + Character through participation in life

By bringing about deep changes in the way we think and feel, then by connecting with the subconscious mind we will excavate negative and inferior complexes that will challenge us to become all we can be.

Let's illustrate the tools that will allow you to carry out such a re-evaluation.

Using the right side of your brain focus on the whole picture, with no limitations, and tapping into the greater sub conscious of what looks good in the ideal world when it comes to you, in fact the Super You. This is an exercise that you will need time for because now we are really focusing on your Ideal Super Self, the person you would like to be, the job you would like to do, the way you want to look, how you want to be with your family and friends, the things you want to achieve. It is taking time to decide what the Super You looks like for if you are to become all that you can be. So take the time now to start modelling your ideal self.

What do you look like?
What is your attitude?
What are your beliefs?
What are your values?
What have you achieved?
Who are your family?
Who are your friends?
What are your interests?
What is your job?
What are your goals?
Where do you want to travel?
Where have you travelled?

Ask yourself as many questions as possible in designing the Super You. In doing this exercise you will gain *Understanding*, which leads to *Enlightenment*, which in turn leads to *Aspiration*.

An important part of this exercise is that you need to write down what good looks like for the Super You as if all the things above are already happening in the present.

Your Super Self has already achieved the things you are planning to do.

WHAT DOES GOOD LOOK LIKE
FOR THE SUPER YOU?

Once you have that picture of your ideal Super Self, let's now use a structured left sided brain activity to order and give you direction.

A Life Needs Analysis can be designed on the self.

Here you define your values, beliefs, goals, training needs and attitude.

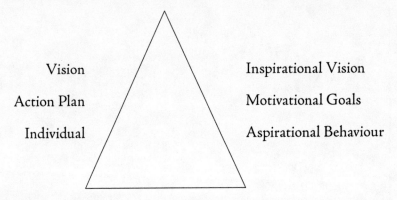

Vision	Inspirational Vision
Action Plan	Motivational Goals
Individual	Aspirational Behaviour

Vision: List your Mission Statement, why you are here, expand on your values and beliefs in life.

Action Plan: What are your goals and a training plan (a programme of self development: knowledge and skills habit forming) in each area of your life?

Individual: Defining your Attitude (Individual Self Concept and Self Esteem) and what is about you that will make a difference?

Once you have re-evaluated you then need to live your beliefs and values. This can be developed further by your self-talk and using positive subliminal affirmations. Your affirmations are easy because they are based on what your Super Self has already achieved. For example,

The Super You earns £60,000 a year.
The Super You has a six pack.
The Super You has been to Australia.
All you need to do is replace the word Super You.

I earn £60000 a year.
I have a six pack.
I have been to Australia.

And then add what the benefit of that is to you.

I earn £60,000 a year which enables me to have all the luxuries I desire
    in life.
I have a six pack which means I feel and look great.
I have been to Australia, which was one of the most fulfilling experiences
of my life.

And then you need to say them each day with a passion and remember the Super You has already achieved them. With this belief your subconscious mind will start to make things happen as surely as you are willing to act in line with your beliefs and your goals.

Everything is becoming. Nothing is. - Plato

You also need to be accountable for your own actions and take complete ownership for your life.

You have said yes to life and you now can picture your ultimate goal, your Super Self.

To become all you can be.

We are what we repeatedly do. Excellence is not an act, but a habit.
- Aristotle

THE SUPER YOU - AFFIRMATIONS

Life Changing Questions

Who are you?

Why are you here?

What do you believe?

What will you choose?

What negative energy is holding you back?

How do you have the freedom to choose your own response?

Will you make the easiest choice?

How do you recognize your self talk? How can you change it?

What does the Super You look like? What does good look like for you?

What would the Super You do in your situation?

> *"Dance like no-one is watching,*
> *Love like you will never be hurt,*
> *Sing like no one is listening,*
> *Live like it is heaven on Earth."* - *William Purkey*

And so he came to the gates of your highest hope and took you in, destined for greatness, bound to life, filled with depth, imparted with sincerity, whole and pure.

'See my unbeliever your higher self, see your destiny to become all you can be, to be true to your greater self, to find freedom in your uniqueness to be genuine, free, and natural.

Now see who you are and rejoice in the moment.

Do you like what you see?'

Summary

1. Negative Energy is not being able to let go of the past, of not being able to make the right response to negative experiences, to wasting energy on feelings of bitterness, anger and resentment, to stagnating within your comfort zone not willing to be stretched.

2. Our identity has many dimensions, which we need to be aware of to be able to make structural changes in our life.

3. An awareness of what our beliefs are about life and why we are here.

4. Life offers choices and it is what we do with the time given to us that matters.

5. We have the freedom to choose our own response to any given situation.

6. We need to be stretched to develop and move beyond our comfort zone.

7. We all have an individual map of the world and to make structural changes in our life we need to analyse our beliefs and values.

8. You have discovered the Super You!

    "A person will worship something, have no doubt about that. We may think our tribute is paid in secret in the dark recesses of our hearts, but it will out. That which dominates our imaginations and our thoughts will determine our lives, and our character. Therefore, it behooves us to be careful what we worship, for what we are worshipping we are becoming." - Ralph Waldo Emerson

Reality Check

In the first part we identified that we all have the option to choose our own subterranean map of the world and that we are normally conditioned to lose but born to win. The fact that we have a choice to decide what our accepted truths will be for our life gives us a freedom to become all we can be. We need to decide exactly what we want from life and to find a deep inner purpose and meaning.

Chapter 4 builds upon those themes.

In identifying what motivates modern man it is important to consider what motivated man in ages gone by, hence our trip back through history, to understand it has been the same man with the same unanswered questions fulfilling their part of the pattern. Although we are all conditioned by the history of mankind and our life experiences, we have the choice to shape our lives. For we all have a deep inner destiny to become all we can be through the fire of our spirit and in being through the essence of our soul.

It is making that deep connection with life.

Chapter 5 revealed the themes of Nietzsche starting with the Will to Power, the idea that mankind should be continually overcoming oneself to improve oneself in working towards a fixed goal, one's highest hope. This was linked to man's ultimate driving source of motivation, the Will to Love, and that it is through the Will to Love that we choose to survive, strive to live life, and improve ourselves. Nietzsche talked of the Super Man and this related to our striving to now become our self-ideal the Super You. In being able to do that we need to say yes to life and yes to the will to love through positive energy, it is the connection and acceptance of life, and it is the realization of one's own highest hope.

Chapter 6 points to becoming all you can be - The Super You.

Interlude 2: Tale in the Making

'People are always blaming circumstances for what they are. I don't believe in circumstances. The people who get on in this world are the people who get up and look for the circumstances that they want...and if they can't find them, they make them.'
- George Bernard Shaw

1

Tale in the Making
(A song in the land of the living)

It's a tale in the making
This land of ours
To a world that's forsaken
In history's lie
For it's in the clouds
That our dreams pass on by
And that we are left to wonder on why

It's a tale in the making
This race of ours
All in the making
Our nature is far
Our ideals pass through ages
From times gone on by
And this beautiful land under the sky

Where in the land of the living
Land of the living dead
Where people pass the past
Of what's been said
Vagrants come and vagrants go

And they will never know
Of our story to be told

The Tale is fresh
The plot is hatched
To find success
The Enigma must last

In each new zone
Lies uncharted seas
And what remains
Is what should be
And to find a way
To this new day

Tale in the making, tale in the making
Unbroken dreams and memories
Tale in the making, tale in the making
Misguided places and territories
Visions and lies and these ecstasies
All in one life
An end to the need

Where in the land of the living
Land of the living dead
Where people pass the past
Of what's been said
Vagrants come and vagrants go
And they will never know
Of our story to be told

If you die will I die?
And if I die will you die
And if I die will it be the end
This tale in the making
In a world that's forsaken

Cannot be mistaken today
You want what I want
And I want what you want
And I want to live forever

All you have to but do is tell the tale, tell the tale
All you have to but do is tell the tale, tell the tale

In each new day
We move away
From the soul of man
And religion of the past

Meaning to life
Has left the earth
Where science has gone
Beyond giving birth

And to understand
Life in this land

Tale in the making, Tale in the making
Unbroken dreams and memories
Tale in the making, tale in the making
Misguided places and territories
Visions and lies and these ecstasies
All in one life
An end to the need

Where in the land of the living
Land of the living dead
Where people pass the past
Of what's been said
Vagrants come and vagrants go
And they will never know
Of our story to be told

For each life that's lived
A tale is told
Of power and love
With silver and gold
And in the end
Each thread will fall
A measure of life
Twilight for all

It's a tale in the making
This mysterious life
Each day brings an awakening
And vision beyond sight
For life is here for you
To make what you will
A tale in the making for me and for you.

2

The Magician's Apprentice

Please will you teach me?

And what would I teach?

You are the master. I wish to learn.

What would you wish to learn?

About magic and about life please.

The magic of life?

Yes.

It always finds a way.

Sorry?

The Buddha sat before a wall and was enlightened. Who would you compare yourself to - the buddha or the wall?

The Buddha, master.

What is this master nonsense? The teaching is not given by the master and there is no master here, only the wall.

What of life?

Where would you start?

Well master, I find there are 2 different types of people in the world, those carrying the world on their shoulders and those who are free as if flying across the horizon.

The children of the dark and the light you speak of...

Yes master, it seems that if I live in a world without hope, without light, without faith, the darkness will surround and engulf the very soul. Down into the fathoms with a falling from grace.

Tell me of this darkness.

It is an energy that burdens the soul and keeps the spirit prisoner. O how I watch the people who never forget the past or who dread the future. O how they are all burdened by every present moment, the jealousy the anger, the bitterness, and resentment are all directed towards the outside world and inevitably directed within. Within their very essence - to the point that they feel choked, like they can't breathe, they can't live. Nothing is their fault - it is the world, the people, their friends, neighbours, family - it's life's fault - not theirs. O how they love to hate and o how they are victimized by life.

It penetrates their sense of the self, their envy destroys their very own soul, lost in a world, born to react and o how they react - hurting others and themselves. And what a cruel world it is - what kind of God would create such a world, such a place, such a hell on Earth. Denizens of the dark side. Losers of the faith. Waybreakers lost in the badlands. Self made purgatory.

And o how they hold on to those negative emotions for life - 'I'll never forgive that bastard' they say 'she's got it coming to her', 'I can't', 'I won't', ' It will never work', 'It's not my fault', 'why me?', 'it's this bloody world not me', 'I have to do this, I have to do that', …..tell me what do they have to do - they don't have to do anything! Negative re-enforcement and conditioning in a self-perpetuating sickness and hell.

And what of the light?

It is the choice to live free, unburdened in an awareness of love and self loving. It is where the rainbow shines brightest in the canderescent feeling of being all one can be. A self contained joy that is found in becoming all one can be. Being true to the self.

O how the angels surround the soul with a spirit that is grounded by choosing one's reaction in all situations to be in harmony with the higher self. It is where daylight begins in the freedom of the choices. It is the sense of all great achievements and it is deeply embedded in humanity's values of worldly righteousness.

O to be surrounded by the light and to free fly like angels upon the earth…

But the voices try to entrap each one of us and take us from the divinity of the light, spiralling down towards the dark night.

Are the voices calling you child?

O how they call - all day and all night tricking, doubting, always criticising thy very soul. The negative chattering of thy own soul's critic continually placing one upon a path of disenchantment.

Don't listen to the voice - like Gollum and the precious, sycophants, bound by the power of the dark voice within. O how the weak are taken by the voice of instinct and desire, of doubting and disarray. Always placing limits upon our day.

How dark is the day when we reactively choose anger, jealousy, desperation, and listen to the doubting voice of negativity - 'You're not good enough - you can't - you will fail - you will fall, you will make a complete fool of yourself.'

No, I cry. No. No. No.

Shall the world lament upon such a solemn sea in a world of disenchantment and pity?

Hmmm, so you have an awareness of the inner voices?

Yes.

And what are they?

The inner critic who causes wanton disarray

Who always makes me doubt my way.

And?

The inner voice who makes the choice.

And?

The greater I who cannot lie

The higher self who knows why

The voice that holds the door to infinity

The keeper of my sanity.

The reactive and proactive choices in the voices of the mind?

Yes my master, it is all within my choices for there lie true riches and wealth. It is the searching for my true self.

How strange, most people never find the time.

Is time the answer master?

Perhaps.

What is the magic of life master?

It does not matter whether you choose to be buddha or the wall in this story - the magic is that you get to choose.

On a light note, would you like a piece of cake?

O yes but not today master.

Please stop calling me master, I'm just a voice in your head....

REACTIVE LIFE	PROACTIVE LIFE
Laziness	Love
Self Hating	Self Loving
Jealousy	Well being
Anger - aggressive	Controlled - assertive
Bitterness	Joy
Resentment	Contentment
Guilt	Freedom
Hatred	Friendliness
Not good enough	Good enough
Feelings of inferiority or arrogance	Inner confidence
Lack of compassion	Compassionate
Pessimistic	Optimistic
Blamer	Aware
Victimised	Partaker of life
I can't	I can
I have to	I want to
Consequences	Benefits
Problems	Challenges

No choice	Choices
Pre determined	Self determining
Hater of life	Lover of life
Tortured Soul	Free Soul
Lack of spirit	Inner spirit

The Soul Will
The Soul Eventuality
It's your choice.

3

No Time

No time to surrender
No time to decay
No time to falter
Upon the way

No time for the weary
No time for the sick
No time for emptiness
No time to tick

Wandering a wasteland
Climbing up a face
Running across a prairie
To find God's Grace
Where angels sing
And lions roar
And children do play
Evermore

No time for forgiveness
No time for hate
No time to fight
The threads of fate

No time to think
No time to be free
No time to be natural
And simply be

Suppressed by a history
Cursed by a shade
Lost in archaic symbols
That slowly fade
Dreaming of paradise
Wishing for space
Upon the plains of the heavens
Where time has no place

Where truth is religion
And love can be
And all are blessed
By harmony
Where no one dies
And no one lies
And no one ever has to hide

Shattered by reality
Broken by life's curse
Chased by the demon
Of nightmares
Where there is

No time to fulfil
No time to breathe
No time to relax

No time to leave

No time to become
No time to love
No time to rise
To high ideals above

Hassled by nature
Harassed to see
Chained by the darkness
Of our mortality

Stressed by work
Trying to be
Chained by the darkness
Of our mortality
Wrong and right
Day and night
No time to understand
Life.

MAKE TIME

Chapter 7: A Code for Life

"It is better to have lived and loved than never to have loved at all."
- - *Lord Tennyson*

In 1953 two unknown scientists claimed they had solved the secret of life. Francis Crick and James Watson pieced together a problem that scientists all around the world were racing to discover and solve. The model they designed was of deoxyribonucleic acid (DNA) and proved that DNA was the carrier of genetic code, the key molecule to heredity and evolution. The beauty of DNA is that it is a self-producing molecule that carries the guidelines for all living things from one generation to the next. A code for life.

Taking this as a metaphor to form the bedrock or foundation of our own personal beliefs system, it is essential to have a code for life that gives us a permanent sense of who we really are. This very foundation is the principles and values we base our life upon. In becoming the Super You it is vital to have a code or principles to base our life upon so that our intentions are not in conflict. This allows us to expend positive energy instead of being troubled by negative energy through a raging of opposite beliefs. It also allows us to move forward with clear line of sight.

Our principles and values should be driven by our inner most feelings about who you want to be. The person within is connected to our DNA principles in life - some of those principles come through hereditary, 'the person you are' and some through conditioning, 'the person you came to be'. For they are deep-rooted principles and values imprinted upon mankind's soul lying between right & wrong, this and that, the soul and the spirit. It is having a code for life or designing our own self-producing DNA code to live by, based on our true beliefs and innermost values.

Let's focus on our principles first.

Imagine you are the Emperor of Rome in Rome's early days - what vision would you have for the eternal city? Would you build a Colloseum or perhaps the Trevi Fountain? Would you build Rome upon high moral principles? The important question here is: **Why?**

The **Why** being our principles – why we act in a certain way, what that is based upon and the why we are here.

The **What** being our Values – what we value most in life and what our beliefs are.

On the basis of the life needs analysis that you have completed on the self, the Vision level is all about having a clear mission statement, understanding why we are here, and having clear measurable goals to get us where we need to go. The bedrock upon which we build the Super You is immovable principles, values and beliefs.

Man is defined by his actions, which are based upon his principles, beliefs and values. This chapter is all about defining your principles. You have set your objectives, you have an understanding of the knowledge and skills you need to improve your life and you have a life winning positive attitude. So what do we do next? We would live and breathe our principles and values in line with our Vision.

ROME was not built in a day but then all roads lead to Rome and there is Rome for everyone in life. There is 'room' for everyone in life, everyone has a place, and it is all part of the pattern; it is understanding the part you play in the pattern and in defining who you are by identifying the principles you choose to live by. It is having a code that is so deeply embedded into our subconscious that we can naturally define our life each day by living in harmony with who we are and where we want to go. The Super You has that sense of direction because the very foundation of our soul is etched upon the landscape of our mind and our reality by living and breathing those principles every waking day.

Let's focus on one such code for life. The beauty is we have the freedom to choose our own.

CODE FOR LIFE: TO LIVE, TO LOVE, TO LEARN.

TO LIVE

To see a world in a grain of sand
And heaven in a wild flower,
Hold infinity in the palm of your hand
And eternity in an hour.
- William Blake

What does it mean 'to live?' What do we mean when we say 'I've lived'? What is the individual implying? That they have done everything? Or is it that we feel we have experienced the variations and the vicissitudes of life to the point that our life is a tale in the making? And not only have we a developed personality but a lifetime of character building experience.

'If only what I knew now I could have known when I was younger...'

If only. But it is learning from experience that shapes us or as John Locke put it 'what we can know'.

What does 'to live' mean? Here are some of the descriptions from the Concise Oxford Dictionary ... Have life...subsist or feed....sustain ones position...spend, pass, experience,... conduct oneself in a specified way... arrange one's habits....survive...escape destruction...enjoy life intensely or to the full....live gaily and extravagantly.

Let's enlighten ourselves. To live is to act; to act is to achieve no matter the outcome, to achieve offers the choice of learning from experience, this in turn builds self-character, through experience, if we choose to positively learn from it.

Write down the major changes you have been through in your life.

(Dating back to early childhood.)

Now go back through those changes and highlight which were the positive and which were the negative changes.

Then consider which of the changes you have learnt from...all of them (Some very consciously but all of them deeply embedded in the subconscious - our mental models and subterranean landscape of the world.)

Scenario: Imagine your life was near perfect, you lived the way you wanted to, had the family and friends, the car, the house and the money. You have the most wonderful life fulfilling moments - the parties, the holidays, the friends, then change takes place - you lose the lot, your partner leaves you, your friends desert you, you lose your job, the car, the house, the money. What would you then do? How would you feel? How would you feel about life?

Would you be grateful for the past (and in the present your health) or be bitter and negative towards life? Would you challenge life and learn by picking up the pieces, or fall at the wayside? Would you choose to be a victim or take accountability?

Belief: To take the good with the bad and learn from it.

If we choose to positively learn from experience it builds self-character and self-belief, which in turn builds self-concept and self-esteem. Now a number of things lead away from this – the more exposure to life changing experience the greater the character – so if we procrastinate and put life off then our self-development is hindered. The taking part in the circle of life is essential to build character and competence. Now I'm not saying that you should go jump out of a plane however it is doing the things that not only will develop the self but will also stretch us beyond our comfort zone.

Life is a gift so it is important not to delay or procrastinate, 'Do it now' is the quote of the day. Some people live to die while really we should all be dying to live.

A girl on one of my courses told us a tragic story that was then immortalized into the Ginger McCain Story. Ginger McCain was a great pilot in the

Second World War flying numerous missions successfully surviving the full length of the war. When the war ended went back home to Cornwall to meet the family and to get a restful nights sleep. The next day his family and friends were holding a party for Ginger in the local pub. After a wonderful day, Ginger left for the evening. He stepped out of the pub around the corner and was run over by the number 10 bus, killing him instantly. All those years flying dangerous missions, Ginger had survived only to be run over by a bus. The moral is that you literally never know what's round the corner – so make the most of every day by making the most of life. Wake up like you meant to and live the perfect day every day.

Belief: You have to live for the present moment and future present moments.

I am sure you have your own stories that make you realize you should make the most of life while you are healthy, while you are living.

It is also about physical action and manifestation. Incidentally it is also important to have an exercise regime that caters for a good physical condition. A healthy mind, a healthy body and vice versa. But then I'm not telling you anything you don't already know.... the Super You is in the best physical and mental condition possible. It is having a positive mindset, which is proactive, and realizing we have the freedom to choose our own response. A lot of people choose to make a negative reaction to everyday situations or on the basis of how other people have treated them. This is where many people become bitter and allow their experiences to shape them instead of learning from experience and shaping their life.

Belief: So it is a call to action! Do things! Be Proactive!

What would you do in these situations?

1. A boy is drowning in an ice-cold lake.

2. The team needs a penalty taker in the last minute.

3. Your friends invite you to do a parachute jump.

4. Your boss invites you to do a big presentation to the directors.

5. You find a purse with £10,000.

Yes, I bet a lot would have taken the money! There are times in life where we have to step out that comfort zone and take risks to develop and build character in line with our values.

Belief: That we want to become all we can be.

Working towards the Super YOU

The Super You takes part - the Super You sees, tastes, smells, hears and touches the richness of life. Are you?

TO LOVE

> *How do I love thee: Let me count the ways,*
> *I love thee to the depth and breadth and height*
> *My soul can reach, when feeling out of sight*
> *For the ends of being and ideal Grace.*
> *I love thee to the level of every day's*
> *Most quiet need, by sun and candlelight.*
> *I love thee freely, as men strive for Right;*
> *I love thee purely, as they turn from Praise.*
> *I love thee with the passion put to use*
> *In my old griefs, and with my childhood's faith.*
> *I love thee with a love I seemed to lose*
> *With my lost saints, - I love thee with the breadth,*
> *Smiles, tears, of all my life!*
> *- Elizabeth Barrett Browning*

Earlier it was mentioned the driving force in life stems from the Will to Love and to love oneself. To regard ourselves highly will build self-esteem and so on. To love and give love (action) results in self-love and an improved self-concept.

> *To love oneself and to give love is all about giving special attention to oneself or another.*

So to love in fact is partly all about giving special attention to detail. Now the opposite to love is not to hate but to not love and to not love is not to give attention or the right attention. The derivative of this is laziness – the will not to act. The will to love is the will to act and provide special attention to detail.

Belief: Man's ultimate motivation is the Will to Love.

Giving attention is all about nurturing our own or another's spiritual growth. It is this attention to detail, in giving love unconditionally, that truly motivates another person.

Belief: Love is about giving special attention.

In life it is definitely better to have loved and lost than never to have loved at all. This saying is in the romantic sense because to love is to act – one cannot lose because it is character building once again. Choosing not to love in life and choosing not to spend time on the detail is to lose.

At all times use love as the driving force.

Belief: The quality of your life depends upon the quality of your love.

This can be described by using the model below.

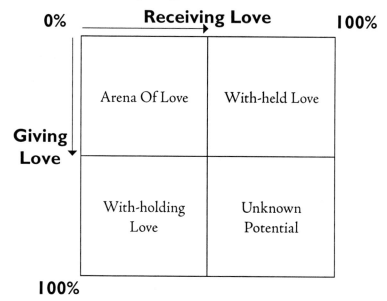

The window above explains that we all have an arena of love within our relationships. The size of the arena depends upon the amount of giving and receiving of love in the relationship. Below the example changes dependent upon who is doing the loving in the relationship.

Example 1: The individual is not loving.

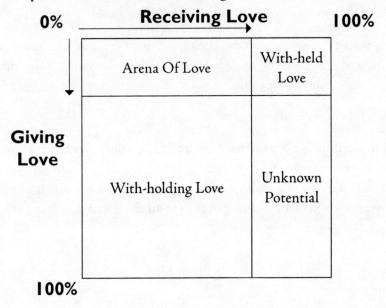

In example 1 the individual is being loved by receiving love but is not loving so what will that create? How does it affect the relationship? There is a lack of trust and the individual who is not loving will either not be in love with the other individual or not be in love with themselves hence not being able to love. By with-holding love the individual is also playing games with the other individual's feelings or could be sitting behind a façade where they have been hurt before and are scared of being hurt again – therefore they are not willing to trust.

Example 2: The individual not being loved

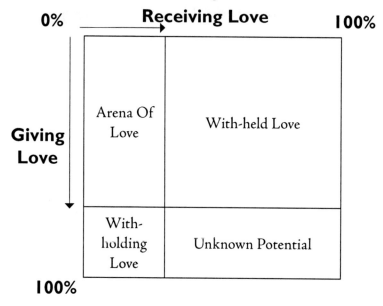

0%   **Receiving Love**   **100%**

**Giving
Love**

Arena Of Love	With-held Love
With-holding Love	Unknown Potential

100%

In example 2 the individual is loving but not loved so how will that affect the relationship? This can result in a lack of trust from the loving person and they will then possibly act insecurely because they are giving and not receiving which gives them doubts that lead to mistrust. In its worst case the individual becomes obsessive or possessive and in this case the person being obsessive or possessive normally has a lack of love for themselves.

In both examples there is a distinct lack of trust in the relationship.

Example 3: Both individuals not loving

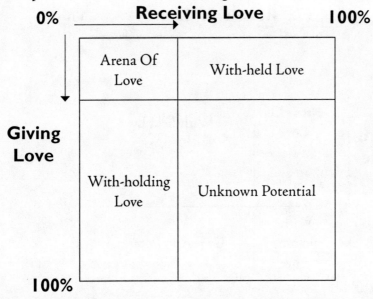

In example 3, both parties are reluctantly giving love, which could be the beginnings of a new relationship, or if this were a long-term relationship it is a very destructive relationship.

In all 3 examples the arena of love is small and needs to be developed. By making the arena of love larger by actively giving and disclosing love then the unknown potential in the relationship can be developed and explored.

In giving love you need to lower any façade you hide behind allowing the individual in to your life and by receiving love, it is not asking for it but being open to it.

In the last example, if the relationship were true to itself then the unknown potential is explored to reach the heights of unconditional love.

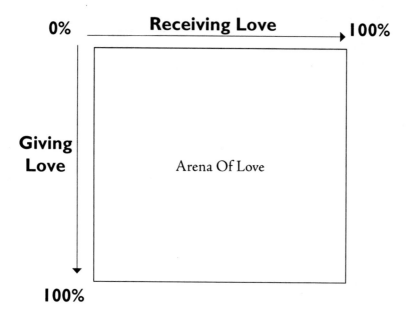

To make any relationship work, both individuals need to use *Understanding and Accountability* to succeed. *Understanding* is the ability to explore the relationship through a high level of trust where both people feel it is possible to seek honest feedback and comfortable to disclose their thoughts and feelings. *Accountability* is for both people to take ownership and responsibility for the relationship realizing that they need to take positive loving action to make the relationship work, hence being able to both give and receive love in an open and unconditional way.

Belief: Use love as the driving force to succeed in life.

MOTIVATIONAL MODEL: THE WILL TO LOVE

POSITIVE MOTIVATION	NEGATIVE MOTIVATION
Unconditional Love Self Sacrifice / Transcendence ↑	The Will to Laziness or Nothing ↓
The Will to Self Actualization / Meaning ↑	No Meaning ↓
The Will to Power / Pleasure / Create ↑	No Power / Pleasure / Creation ↓
The Will to Self Realization ↑	No Realization ↓
The Will to Belong ↑	No Belonging ↓
The Will to Security ↑	No Security ↓
The Will to Survival ↑	No Will to survive ↓
The Will to Love	No Will to live

The above model links to Maslow's hierarchy of needs but the difference is that man's ultimate source of motivation is the will to love. It is love of the self that drives the will to survive, secure, belong, self realize, seek power/pleasure, to create, to find meaning and to transcend our self, our will to love is driven by our self-love based on our self-concept and self esteem. If we have high a self-concept in line with our self-esteem then higher up the model you can go. The opposite is the will to nothing or to not love or to laziness in which case we quickly move in the opposite direction.

Belief: You have the freedom to choose your own response and actions in any given situation!

Real love is to be genuine and is given proactively.

RELATIONSHIPS DEFINED BY THE TALE OF ARTHUR & LANCELOT

Here is a very simple explanation of most people's relationships. Arthur Pendragon, the boy King who wields Excalibur from the stone, is a lot like Lancelot in the first part of the story. He is the White Knight in shining armour- frivolous, adventurous and a free spirit. But Arthur marries Guinevere and becomes a King of values that he will live and die by. Arthur in a sense becomes plain but what Arthur is as the King is consistent, true, always there, genuine, honest and faithful. What more could a woman ask for? He rules his kingdom with his heart and he creates a home so grand for Guinevere in Camelot.

But then along comes Lancelot, the bravest, most courageous and exuberant knight. He is not the white knight but the knight in shining armour. Lancelot is attractive because he is a free spirit and has a sense of adventure; he's volatile, and changeable. Women tend to love him because he is a charmer and always in high spirits but he is unreliable and lives for himself.

In the story both Arthur and Guinevere love Lancelot, he quickly becomes Arthur's most brave Knight and trusted friend, whilst secretly Guinevere lusts after the adventurous Lancelot. For years Guinevere keeps her love for Lancelot to herself and Lancelo,t who can have any woman he chooses, will love only his Queen. When at last Lancelot cannot help himself any longer they meet in secret union in the woods only to be found by Arthur.

The sad part is that Guinevere loves both Arthur and Lancelot.

What does the tale explain? Firstly that most women fall in love with the Lancelot in men because when they meet their partner he is free and single and acts in a very similar to Lancelot. So the attractiveness for a lot of women is the unreliable, exuberant free qualities and spirit. After a set amount of time (which differs within each relationship) a woman decides to change her man into a more reliable, consistent, honest, faithful and less adventurous one. She tries to turn him into Arthur. Sound familiar?

Because really it is Arthur that a woman wants (until she has him) because unfortunately, for a lot of men, when they become like Arthur, most women then miss, or want a man to still be like Lancelot. So, relationships can become boring and dull to the woman but the man who is Arthur becomes set in his ways and even more consistent in fatherhood. (He forgets to show her the same quality of attention he did when they met and she notices this, which in turn becomes a form of rejection.)

Now for a woman who has Arthur when she sees or meets a Lancelot there is an instant attraction. Now if that woman strays to start a new relationship with Lancelot she then attempts to turn him into Arthur but if this Lancelot does not want to become an Arthur or if it is just not in his nature then Lancelot he remains. And a lot of the time the lady wants Arthur back. The travesty of life!

Some women just want an Arthur or a Lancelot but that also is part of the problem because the man himself can change. The cliché is that most men start as Lancelot when single and become like Arthur when in a relationship or become married.

*For some women, it is the **falling in love** with Lancelot and the not **being in love** with Arthur that they crave, and so will go from relationship to relationship.*

The story has been told with women as the example but it can be just the same case for men. For just as the man falls in love with Guinevere does he then take Guinevere for granted? He fails to listen to her attentively like when they first met and fails to provide the same attention and thrill that Guinevere requires. Generally men do not try to change Guinevere but they may do through a lack of attention through ignorance and considerate action. It is the feeling of being taken for granted that changes Guinevere into his mother!

Arthur (men) falls into the building of Camelot and then spends more time with the Knights of the Round Table (his mates) either upon quests to free the land (nights out) or playing and watching jousting (his favourite sport). His lack of attention and lack of detail shown towards Guinevere means that she now, instead of being the attractive and fair maiden, becomes a nag and less attractive through her tentative demands.

This is where Arthur's roaming eye is attracted by the Lancelot in women and sometimes because he is King he feels he has a divine right to taste. But when Arthur starts upon the tasting road, once again he becomes Lancelot.

An Arthur is only true when he is true to himself.

Belief: Love is all about being true to yourself or another.

Love then is an action and it is the action of giving special attention to detail when it comes to yourself or another person. If we treat each person as we expect to be treated ourselves then that's a start but to achieve the realms of genuine love would be to treat each person better than we expect to be treated ourselves, or to consider how they would want to be treated…it is to go that extra mile.

If we go that extra mile with another person how motivated do they become!

It is nurturing our own or the other person's spiritual growth, which means we want the best for yourself or the other person. We are not willing to hold yourself or that other person back. Sometimes, by giving love and allowing the other person to be all they can be means letting that person go because if we did not we would be stifling that persons spiritual growth. Self-sacrifice is the highest form of genuine and unconditional love.

Although we can't love another person more than we love ourselves, the more love we give the more we will receive. In giving the intention is not to receive more back, it is the satisfaction that we are becoming all we can be, it is the feeling of inner contentment, through understanding, enlightenment, aspiration, accountability, action and achievement.

To give love is to give love because like attracts like and if you have that mindset then your life will be filled with love; don't think to give love is to receive love because the intention is wrong. I would think more along the lines that if you give love then the other person will then give love through their self esteem being higher and it may be that they give it to themselves first.

You may now be thinking, I have loved someone and they have taken all the love and given none back and now you're not willing to give love. If that is the case you will definitely not receive the love you are after. Having the type of mindset that the world is against you will be damaging because your glass will always be half empty and so will your life. The world is really conspiring to do you good and if you think that way then the world will be a better place. If you are willing to share your love and give special attention you will then start to notice the meaningful coincidences sent by your inner guide because you will be more open to good things happening to you which are all part of the pattern.

Belief: The world is conspiring to do you good.

Love is all about taking accountability for our actions. Once again we are in control of our life so what are you going to do with the time given to you?

> *My Friend, and thou, our Sister! We have learnt*
> *A different lore: we may not thus profane*
> *Nature's sweet voices, always full of love*
> *And joyance! 'Tis the merry Nightingale*
> *That crowds, and hurries, and precipitates*
> *With fast thick warble his delicious notes,*
> *As he were fearful that an April night*
> *Would be too short for him to utter forth*
> *His love chant, and disburthen his full soul*
> *Of all its music!*
> *Samuel Taylor Coleridge – The Nightingale*

TO LEARN

'The unexamined life is not worth living.' - Socrates

What is learning? What do we already know through heredity, is their some form of universal knowledge that we are born with? Can we all tap into the collective unconscious? Or perhaps we are born with a blank slate ready to write our own epic novel and tale?

Belief: Every life is an epic tale in the making.

The fact is we are learning every minute of every day from the day we are born. There are two distinct types of learning, the every day learning from experience and the active learning such as reading a book, attending school, college, university. The two types of learning are reactive learning to life and proactive learning to actively develop ourselves. Although the reverse can happen in both cases a child goes to school to proactively learn but learns more from the reactive experience of going to school. Also in life we can choose to take risks to proactively stretch ourselves, which heightens the reactive experience to the situation.

There are four kinds of remembering in life that help us to learn Recognition, Recall, Reproduction and Performance. These link to the cycle of learning by experience, which is having an experience, reviewing the experience, concluding from the experience and planning the next steps.

To learn is to develop the self and learn by experience. Even if there were a library of infinite knowledge and even if you were to live forever there would always be something to learn; it is understanding our preferred style of learning and continuing to take action.

Learning by experience and learning itself offer the proactive opportunity to improve oneself; to strive towards self-understanding and work towards a purposeful goal or meaning.

Belief: Everything happens for a reason and we should learn from it.

If we truly believe the world is conspiring to do us good, that we are saying yes to life with a high self concept and esteem, and we are sharing our love by giving special attention to the world, then our powers of intuition will be heightened. Some people are gifted with intuition naturally but how many listen to what it is trying to tell us? Your intuition and the meaningful coincidences are part of the pattern for you.

Belief: You shape your own destiny and your destiny shapes you.

That is the ambivalence and riddle of life.

What is important is that we learn from every experience to become all that we can be; the eternal cycle of being and becoming.

A return to classical ways is needed in that the teaching of philosophy and morality in schools along with personal development studies is needed. If we have lived through the last millennium in the discovery of science then the next will be the re-discovery of the spirit and the soul resulting in a spiritual renaissance. In the last thousand years we have believed that we are an object in the world; that the universe does not revolve around the earth, that it is possible that life is purely down to chance and that we have evolved from apes. We have lost our myths in the relinquishing consistent faith in religion and our belief has been shattered by so many religious wars and the abuse of religion by terrorism. We have the freedom to choose our own religion (and that choice is now vast) and we have the freedom not to believe. As with medicine the patient is not just to be operated upon or diagnosed by the doctor as an object, life has evolved and it is the belief that the patient holds the key to their own recovery within their own belief system. Our lost beliefs have meant a loss of the soul and a psychosomatic plague that has spread across mankind in the form of neuroses and personality disorders. It is a modern crisis that has spread across the globe with disproportionate wealth, over population and fearful trepidation of the future by all levels of age. There is a distinct lack of belief in mankind…and the human spirit.

It is the rediscovery of ourselves beginning with love of the self that will enable us to give love out into the world. Once we have achieved that, we will learn to live with one another respecting another's life and religious views. It is having consistent principles with a defined cause and living by that code which will give us our highest hope.

What you sow so shall you reap – learning proactively to improve the self.

> *Belief: Everything happens for a reason – what goes around comes around.*

It is fundamentally important that we then take action and live like a warrior would live - by the code.

> *Belief: There is no such thing as failure when you are acting upon your principles and values.*

To learn is to love the self and it is character building because with learning comes self-growth and application.

Let's cry together "To Live, To Love, To Learn" and ride the sands of time together!

So why is character so important? It's the powerful combination of learning from experience and using ones principles and values (feelings, beliefs). It's having a meaning worth working towards that makes character and character, in turn, enables you to become all you can possibly be.

Every person should have a code for life. The concept is similar to having theme tunes within films, i.e. like in Rocky with 'Eye of the Tiger'. Not only do I have a code for life but also my own theme tunes that I play to accompany my tale in the making.

I am sure you have had certain songs represent experiences in your life. Perhaps when you have first fallen in love or when you have split up with someone or music you grew up with or music from a movie. The music probably represented times that you were happy or sad which you identify with because it represents your identity or inspires you to work or train hard.

Music is an empowering way to add drama and inspiration to your life.

Just as music and exercise go together, imagine your life as a movie and find your own soundtrack for your life as an epic motion picture and live each day like it is...

A TALE IN THE MAKING.

YOUR PRINCIPLES DEFINITION

YOUR VALUES
DEFINITION

YOUR BELIEFS
DEFINITION

Life Changing Questions

What are your principles in life? How do you know?
What do you really value? What are your values?
Which of the above principles and values are your own?
What risks are you willing to take in life to stretch?
How are you stretching yourself?
What is the Arena of love like for yourself?
For your relationships?
How are you learning and developing yourself?
What are your theme tunes in life?
What is your tale in life about?

"We don't see things as they are, we see them as we are."
- Anais Nin

'What do you live by my child? What is the basis for your life? For this your life's tale what will you write? For how the days pass and every day is a lesson in life, in living, in loving, in learning and what do you learn? What do you learn about yourself and about this life? What do you choose to give attention to? What is your passion? What is your love? What are your dreams? Your realities? Where is your home? Where is your quest? Where is your destiny? Where are you going my friend North, South, East or West? Where and why?

Summary

1. It is better to have loved and lost than to never have loved at all.

2. There is Rome for everyone.

3. To take the good with the bad and learn from it.

4. You have to live for the present moment and future present moments.

5. It is a call to action.

6. We want to become all that we can be.

7. Man's ultimate motivation is the will to love.

8. Love is about giving special attention.

9. The quality of your life is dependent upon the quality of your love.

10. Use love as the driving force to succeed in life.

11. You have the freedom to choose your response in any situation.

12. Love is all about being true to yourself and another.

13. The world is conspiring to do you good.

14. Every life is an epic tale in the making.

15. Everything happens for a reason.

16. You shape your destiny and your destiny shapes you.

'TO LIVE, TO LOVE, TO LEARN'
You have the freedom to choose your own code
for life based upon your principles.

"Every man is the architect of his own fortune." - Salust

Chapter 8: The Character

'Far better to dare mighty things, to win glorious triumphs, even though checkered by failure, than to take rank with those poor spirits who neither enjoy nor suffer much, because they live in the grey twilight that knows not victory, nor defeat.' – Theodore Roosevelt

---

Character? What is it about character or a character we all love? Is it that the person embodies or accentuates life? That our fascination is through the stories they tell? The life they have lived? Or is it their talents or perhaps their humour? Their energy and vitality?

In life the choices we make shape the character we are. Our life's tale or very own motion picture can be what we want it to be - whether that be of epic proportions or slick documentary or a sensual landscape of serenity. In being all that we can be the result is you, the character.

I asked a lady to write a book, she said no-one would read it if she did.

I asked her again to do it for me, she said I would not read it either.

I asked her a third time to do it for herself. 'Oh,' she said 'For me?'

I replied: 'Who cares if they choose not to read - you chose to write. Have you the inner character?'

In defining your character you are literally appreciating how appealing you are to yourself and other people. It is having a sense of who you are, who you want to be and an awareness of how other people see you. In looking in the mirror you can define your own character by realizing the real you. We have already discussed the Super You, which is your ideal self. The question has to be when it comes to defining your character what is the difference between you as you know yourself to be and the Super You.

It is also interesting to consider how others may see you – what type of character or lack of character they perceive you to have.

Leaving that to one side for a moment...

If there is such a thing as Heaven and we are all angels of the Lord, then what would your idea of Heaven be? In John Martin's epic painting the plains of heaven are an esoteric lush green landscape filled with angels and blue waters as clear as our souls. What would your idea of an ideal heaven be?

And what if you were God and you had the opportunity to shape the Earth and you could decide upon the universal laws of mankind. How would you shape the world and what would those laws be?

So you have chosen your ideal heaven and if you were God what would you shape? What rules would you make? Are there any similarities between your Heaven and Earth? What laws have you decided upon? That everyone is equal, that the wealth is equal and that there would be universal contentment and happiness? If so do you realize that there would be no free will, that we would be destined to be moderate, average, that we would never excel or dream. That this form of homeostatic world would lead to divine discontentment and unhappiness?

Or would you leave the world as it is because you are a believer in the circle of life, or perhaps you created a peaceful world blessing all with immortality - Heaven on Earth!

What would the consequences be?

If you have a conscience it is natural to want to create a world of equal opportunity where there is no war, famine, disease. It is an appreciation that there are people worse off than you and that you want to help.

If you really wanted the world to be that way the question I have is 'What are you doing about it?'

And if you are doing nothing - then surely you accept it the way it is.

Because if you don't accept it the way it is and you have just created the vision - the bigger picture a better world then what steps will you take to create that world? Are you willing to sacrifice the self in pursuit of the divine good - if so then you have my blessing - not that you need it? There are few angels left in this world and it's a shame how quickly we forget our wings.

You can choose to accept the world the way it is or you can do something to change the way it is. You decide.

We are born in a world of being and becoming to become all that we can be and develop life character.

'The essence actually lies in both the struggle and the victory.'

So why is character so important? And what do we mean by character?

What is Character?

Dictionary definition…

1. The collective qualities or characteristics that distinguish a person or thing.

2. A moral strength (e.g. a weak character).

3. Reputation (e.g. a good reputation).

4. A person in a novel or play.

5. A person especially eccentric or outstanding.

6. A symbol or distinctive mark.

A person who develops character carries distinctive marks and symbols as if living in a novel, with each life being a tale in the making; we judge the character of the person.

Character definition:

Character is built upon the principles, values and beliefs you choose.

Character is all about the feeling of the spirit and the spirit of feeling. It is the synthesis of the choices of the mind and the feeling of a greater sense of the world. It is built upon the values we choose and it is being in line with the universal values of integrity that exist within the collective unconscious of us all. Our deep feelings generate and help us to create our own values and belief system. It is this value driven automatism that supports the very foundation of everything we do. As already stated it is how you feel about yourself and the world around you. These beliefs are encased within our values to give you true character.

Character building is to learn from experience.

We are shaped by the world around us from childhood to adulthood and we shape ourselves by learning from experience. It is by stretching ourselves that we build character, from both the good and the bad experiences we have faced or are due to face. Our character forms in our response to those experiences.

Character is built by modelling the world and other people.

Character is also shaped by the external stimuli we choose to model into our everyday life.

Character is formed from a life of many experiences.

The foundation of the spirit is born in the home – that form of modelling when young gives us the strength of character by identifying with our own.

Character building is to inaugurate the power to accept what we are and change what we can.

Being value driven is to become accountable for our beliefs, shaping those beliefs and holding those values / beliefs firm in the mind each day. It gives us a strong sense of identity and enables us to act with integrity in line with our own table of beliefs and to live by our own code, our chosen principles.

Where do we get our values? From childhood we learn what is right and wrong and through different encounters our experience teaches us what to value the most. Values are partly taught and the rest learned from experience. Undoubtedly those who brought us up have a major part to play in shaping our beliefs system and it is through these shared values that eventually we reach adolescence when we start to then shape our own. From there we then form our inherent ethics, we are influenced by friends, books, the media, in general by the law tables and morals of ethical code that exist within society. We are raised by conformity and conditioned by culture so that if we are brought up by a certain culture whose parents believe in charity, truth and kindness there will be a very good chance the child will share those values when they grow up. However we know that is not always the case and it depends how quickly the child progresses to maturity.

Here is the beauty of evolution and the spiritual revolution that we are embarking upon. With each generation, the next generation build upon the values of the last, taking them to the next step of moral ground.

Our values have changed from shared values within the community to individual values, and with those values come accountability and responsibility.

So we inherit our parents' or adopted parents' beliefs and then sculpt those beliefs further to define greater values based on the family moral code. But this code has naturally been passed down through the generations; some families are only just in the beginning of their code whilst others are highly evolved. Although Christianity's moral code is based on the Ten Commandments, this code of universal truths existed long before Moses. I use the word truth, because it is an inescapable truth that you cannot deny, for example, that man deep down knows that it is wrong to kill another human being. These universal values have been passed down through the generations. To think in moral terms it means that we must be rational beings to decide reasons for and against doing or willing accordingly.

> *"Act only according to that maxim by which you can at the same time will that it should become a universal law." - Immanuel Kant – A Critique of Pure Reason*

Quite simply, if we do not believe that a certain value should be adopted as a universal rule and acted upon by everyone then it should not form part of our beliefs system and moral code. It is a fact that there are conditions of morality that we all have to abide by as rational beings and it is these universal truths that we recognize through our thoughts and feelings about what is right and what is wrong.

Mankind's universal truth is that he reasons as a sentient being. This alone creates a dualistic world where he rationally decides on good and evil, right and wrong, left and right. It is through this rationality that he comes to singular truths that are eternal to the creation of mankind and offer meaning within our boundaries of time and space because they exist beyond time and space.

We are trapped by our conditioning to the fact we think that we experience everything in life through time and space. Our values are universal because of their sheer righteousness of what we truly feel to believe. It is this inner character that endorses the intuition of universal possibilities.

> *"Act in such a way that you always treat humanity, whether in your own person or in the person of any other, never simply as a means, but always at the same time as an end."* Immanual Kant – Critique of Pure Reason

This speaks for itself. Treat other people how we expect to be treated ourselves. This formal rule of conduct covers all ethical choices.

Now you might challenge this by saying that you can't prove what is right and wrong by reason alone, especially since Hume said 'reason is the slave of the passions' but there are inescapable truths that deep inside we know to be right or wrong, and it is this reasoning that allows us to realize that it is wrong to become a slave to our ego, greed or desires.

It is all about having the inner character that has been archetypal throughout history. Through the generations the human race has evolved through their deep religious beliefs and values of what is right and wrong. These universal beliefs are the foundation that shapes our inner character. It is this inner character that gives us real strength to live this life through our choices and the driving force the will to love.

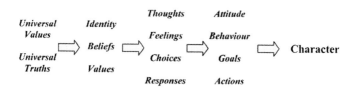

Within the self such Universal truths and values can be built in to our own values system giving us a firm sense of identity. This allows us to use our thoughts and feelings to make the best choices and responses to any given situation. It is all about being true to our self, defining our attitude and behaviour, having clear goals and taking consistent action. It is this that develops character through the choice of spiritual development that stretches the spirit and the soul; the spirit being the life force and the soul our eternal and true identity.

At the end of the day it is our self who decides our own values and through practical reason we evaluate our own beliefs about our self, society and the world around us. It is our conscience that connects with the universal. It is realising that we are in control through free will and that we decide to have values that will shape our self as a character not to be conditioned by society and culture or to be conditioned by childhood fears or negative beliefs. We choose to shape our own world.

They say a leopard can't change its spots; the animal itself can't but in the context of the saying a leopard can. It is through a choice of free will. We can decide to choose an alternative course of action. Breaking the habit is the hard part and that's why, as Covey stresses, we need to go back to our values/beliefs to be able to make the right choices that will reinforce the necessary action.

In shaping your own character it is not the thing in itself but how it appears to you. So if we design our own scripts to determine who we are and what we feel about our self and marry those scripts with a deep understanding of our universal beliefs that will give us the power to act with integrity and attract positive situations into our life.

Why is character so important?

'Like attracts like.' It is character that people buy into because it's a fact that people buy people first. We all buy attitude. Relating this to the market place we all like doing business with people we like and it's a fact that people want to be associated with winners. People love character of the universal kind! How do we gain character? As we have said through being in line with our universal truths and then through life experiences. At the end of the day we are all motivated by opportunities that allow us to grow, however we all tend to dislike stepping out of our comfort zone.

Some people are born risk takers, most are not.

To develop self-character we need to empower our self to take risks. It is a fact when we meet new people we are attracted to the interesting characters who have had plenty of life experience and usually a tale or two stories to tell. The only way to develop character is to jump in at the deep end.

To live, to love, to learn. We are in control of our life, we can proactively choose our response to any given situation, so empower yourself to having life experiences. We have to do wrong to learn what is right but if we play safe all the time how boring would the world become. Now I'm not saying go the casino and gamble your house away, keep the house I would. But go out and enjoy the richness of life by experiencing it.

Nor does it mean you have to go out and see the world by travelling the height and depth of the planet. Go and explore your own world, where ever that may be. For some, it is the external world of people; for others, the inner world of ideas. For others, being close to their family; to another, travelling to the other side of the world....whatever enables you to become all you can be.

Let's go out into the world together, to live, to love, to learn, because the quickest way to grow is to have a go! You have to be in it to win it! So get out there and do the things you want to do the most, in fact do the things that would have the greatest effect on your life that perhaps you are not doing now. And remember not everything that is wrong is right to do but sometimes you have to do wrong to learn what is right.

Below I have defined how to shape character in a model. This shows the four main contributions to developing character as being your beliefs and values, a willingness to be stretched and take risks, a sense of purpose through clear goals and the partaking of life experiences which shape you through learning from experience.

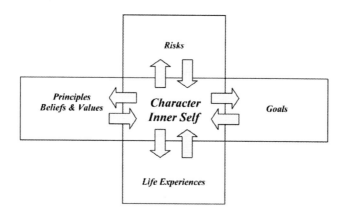

A strong character has a sense of inner direction and is clear on his or her path in life. They believe in themselves and in doing so work and develop themselves with great passion and vigour.

To transfer that concept over to the work place most companies fail to generate such belonging and belief in the soul of the company because they have no soul. No soul = no belief = no commitment to the cause = cause and effect or lack of cause with effect.

Companies need to fully realize that if individuals do not believe the company has a soul then they may work hard for personal benefit but they will never be truly committed to the company. Some individuals will find meaning and belonging with a company but that can be due to a lack of meaning and belonging in their own life.

How many socialize only through work, so work becomes their entire life. Here is a classic example of consequences. If you choose to totally devote yourself to your job then there are bound to be consequences, especially if you have a family. Personally, I work to live, not live to work. It is about having a work/life balance. It is important to be part of and take part in life whilst maintaining an awareness of the consequences of your actions. This can be summed up by the following equation.

Risk x Benefits – Consequences = If one should take risk/action.

Quite simply, any risk you take is worth taking dependent upon how great the benefits are weighed up against the consequences. If the consequences outweigh the benefits, is it worth taking action? The final deciding factor will then be our conscience or our willingness to take the risk. Or our inner character will make the commitment to take action based on our values and goals.

What we are talking about here is the commitment to follow your leader into battle because the soul cause is so great that the choice makes itself, or to actually take your troops into battle, leading by example and demonstrating belief in cause. Too many companies are dragging their employees around the world on the pursuit of globalization but clearly do not have the values or a believable cause.

An example of the greatest of soul causes is the protection of your family, the reason why most people go to work. However, in times of danger to protect the land, the country, the flag, from evil conquerors, is not even a dwelling point for most people. It is a universal cause.

Transferring that to a work model, the individual needs to share the company's beliefs and values, and believe the company is credible and valid. It does what it says on the tin. Therefore the company cares about the development of each individual's character and competence through ongoing development and training, and career viability. Also the individual finds sense of purpose in the company's cause which transforms the idea of a company being a place of hard line results to one of spiritual enlightenment, belonging and contentment. The company cares about me; I am a truly valued individual on a physical, emotional, mental and spiritual level.

When I believe in the Soul of the Company then it opens up the door to greater possibilities. When I believe in my own cause, then anything is possible.

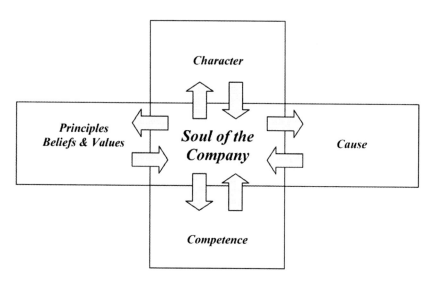

So you should now have your life's code through defining your principles, values and beliefs in line with your soul's cause.

WHAT IS YOUR CAUSE IN LIFE?

What then is the aim for the character or to develop character? In keeping with a higher hope, it is developing the character of the Super You. To do that the whole character in this modern day and age would develop the whole person paradigm of Intellectual Intelligence (IQ), Physical Intelligence (PQ), Emotional Intelligence (EQ), Psychological Intelligence (PSYQ) and Spiritual Intelligence (SQ). These five intelligences are essential for the healthy growth of any individual.

Intelligence	Whole Person	Action	Content	Levels
PQ	Body (Doing)	To Live	Health & Well Being	Physical
IQ	Mind (Knowing)	To Learn	Learning & Understanding	Mental
EQ	Heart (Being)	To Love	Relationships & Love	Emotional
PSYQ	Will (Spirit)	To Become	Goals & Self Ideal	Psychological
SQ	Soul (Being Human)	To Be	Spiritual Growth & Meaning	Spiritual

It is developing character as a complete person on a physical, mental, emotional and spiritual level. PQ is our instinct to survive - it is our health and well being in a situation. It is what we physically do, hence represented by the Body and Doing. IQ is our mental growth and development through learning. It is our ability to understand the situation - represented by Mind and Knowing. EQ focuses on relationships, our emotions and the emotions of others and it is how we react in the situation. On an emotional level, it is represented by Heart and Being i.e. who we are being when we are doing what we know. PSYQ is our psychological self, how our self-concept and self-esteem line up with our self-ideal, which is represented by will and the spirit to become. On a psychological level it is the freedom to choose who we are at any given time. SQ is how we find meaning, act with integrity, and our contribution on a deeper level - it is actually identifying we have a choice as to whether we want to be in the situation, change it, create a better one - represented by Soul and Being Human. In being human it is living by universal values, acting with integrity, living to higher quality of life.

> "Your true character is revealed in the clarity of your convictions, the choices you make, and the promises you keep. Hold strongly to your principles, and refuse to follow the currents of convenience. What you say and do defines who you are, and who you are...you are forever."

Life Changing Questions

What is your definition of character?
What is your real character? The 'you' you know yourself to be?
What is the Super You's Character?
How do others perceive you as a character?
What was your idea of Heaven?
What was your ideal Earth like?
Is there a difference? What are you doing about it?
What are your parent's beliefs? What are your own?
How do they differ? Why do they differ?
What do you feel is right or wrong deep down?
What are your universal beliefs?
What habits do you want to break?
What risks are you willing to take?
What is your cause in life?
What makes an inspirational character?

> "Our lives begin to end the day we become silent about things that matter." -Dr. Martin Luther King Jr

> Balanced above the precipice he holds your soul between scales of longitude and latitude to see how heavy your lot has become. In magnitude he sings before all:

'What measure of creature is this to have no character, to not give, to not help, to not try, to not risk, to not cry, and not laugh? What measure of man calls himself partaker of life who lives no life and worse lives no life and learns not. Beholder of distance and disruption, to take no accountability or responsibility, locked in battle with demon, incantation and spell, wanton and disarray, madness of tranquillity, prison called mind, voices, echoes, swirling mist, violent. That is no life to be lived without shape, without character, without risk, O no my child do not make the easiest choice, instead find wholeness in the realm of life's challenges, life's risks, life's journey and know you are destined for greatness and for your own eventuality. Be your own white knight in valour, honour and integrity. True to your vision, universal in your action, a character whose tale needs to be told.

What is your name? What does it mean? What story will it tell?'

Summary

1. We are all attracted to character.

2. In life the choices you make shape the character you are.

3. In appreciating your own character and your own map of the world (Heaven/ Earth in the exercise) shapes your choices.

4. Character is built upon the values you choose.

5. Character building is to learn by experience.

6. Character is built by modelling the world and other people.

7. Character is formed from a life of many experiences.

8. We all have universal values.

9. We all buy attitude and character.

10. To build character you need to take risks and take part in life.

11. Our inner character shapes our cause in life and the two go hand in hand.

12. Whole person character is a measure of IQ/PQ/EQ/PSYQ/SQ.

"The destiny of man is in his own soul." - Herodotus

Chapter 9: A Way of Life

"Your vision will become clear only when you look into your heart. Who looks outside, dreams. Who looks inside, awakens."
- Carl Gustav Jung

To take risks we simply empower ourselves to take the first step and continue to take those steps. In putting ourselves in a position to win in life we have to accept that sometimes we could lose. Empowerment of the self is linked to our own self-assertion and having the self discipline to continue with best practice. To be able to empower ourselves, we have to have a clear understanding of the goal or target. To be self-motivated and believe in cause, we need to have a sense of purpose and a goal. This means that we need to have clear goals that are measurable and achievable.

Here is an exercise on setting goals.

Using the right side of the brain and thinking with no limitations write down your goals. Think big but in line with your hearts content.

Now using the left side of your brain do the same except only write down what you think would be achievable in the next 6-12 months.

When setting any goals in life we should always start with the right brain by thinking of the whole picture. It is really thinking about exactly what you want from life and what we want the end outcome to be without limitations. With this holistic vision you need to strongly visualize your goals and then write them down. Once you have these main goals think about why you really want to achieve them and how it makes you feel now and what it will feel like when you have achieved them in the future. It is all about captivating that feeling and it is a feeling of rightness and of becoming everything you can.

Once you have clearly visualized, you can then use the left side of your brain to help you achieve the vision. Now don't listen to the left with its limitation setting and negative comments. Use the logic of the left to its best ability to break down your goals. The best way to do this is to write or mind map your main goals into areas of your life that matter most. Below is a model for how you can order your life in to manageable areas to give you clarity of focus.

Psychological - Self Image	Who you are – comparison of the real you and the super you – this is your self-concept, self-esteem and self-ideal (PSYQ)
Physical - Self Health & Well being	Your health and fitness – what shape you are in, exercise and diet (PQ)
Social / Emotional - Self-Belonging	Your relationships - with friends, family, social groups and your emotional state (EQ)
Mental - Self Development	Your self-development – learning and developing yourself mentally (IQ)
Occupational - Work	Your status, occupation and career development (PSYQ/PQ/EQ/IQ/SQ)

| Spiritual - Home |

Your spiritual self – the person you are when you are on your own, your deeper and spiritual connections with life (SQ)

You should split your life into manageable chunks with the key areas, for example, home, work, health and well-being, self-development, self-image and social/emotional. Have up to six key areas to focus on and to make it personal.

An explanation of how the model works for me is as follows.

| Psychological - Self Image |

Self Image for me is all about how I feel and look. This is built from the will to love with self-love being the driver. In saying yes to life I am saying yes to becoming all that I can be. It is state of mind and the ability to change state.

| Physical - Self Health & Well being |

This is all about my health and fitness, going the gym, training, the sports I play, nutrition and diet. This builds on the first were a healthy body balances a healthy mind and vice versa.

| Social / Emotional - Self-Belonging |

This is family and friends, social arrangements and lifestyle. It is also the belonging to any club or organization. It is also our freedom to choose our emotional state.

| Mental - Self Development |

Self-Development is all about learning and developing the mind. This is study, reading, qualifications, building your knowledge base.

| Occupational - Work |

This includes career, finances, money, etc., so really what I do for a job, my career expectations, and my financial situation.

Spiritual - Home

This is the person I am when on my own at home and my surroundings within the home. It is also my deeper beliefs about life and my inner connections with all that is spiritual.

The great thing is I can change the order of priority to suit me when most needed. All are equally important.

So how can we make this really work for you? Firstly I need you to divide your life into six sections at the most.

YOUR SIX KEY AREAS OF LIFE

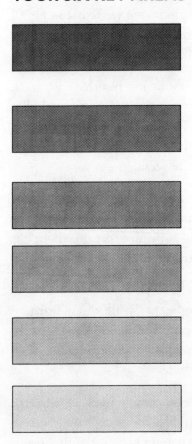

Now follow these steps to clearly define your life's goals.

Step 1: Mission Statement

For each area you need to decide exactly what you want, so what you set yourself are a number of things. The objectives come first, so have a good think of what you really want from each area. Then for each area write a mission statement, which captures exactly what you are setting out to achieve.

Step 2: The Super You

Then for each area ask yourself what would the Super You have achieved and visualize this as being real. So describe what the Super You has achieved and complete the vision section. Finally write your own positive affirmations at this stage as if they have happened e.g., if the Super You earns £60k a year then write *I earn £60k a year.*

Complete your own versions over the next few pages.

Area 1:

Mission Statement

Positive Affirmations

Vision

Area 2:

Mission Statement

Positive Affirmations

Vision

Area 3:

Mission Statement

Positive Affirmations

Vision

Area 4:

Mission Statement

Positive Affirmations

Vision

Area 5:

Mission Statement

Positive Affirmations

Vision

Area 6:

Mission Statement

Positive Affirmations

Vision

Step 3: How do you rate yourself?

In each area, if the Super You was 10 out 10 all the time then how do you presently rate? Give yourself a score for each area. A 10 would mean that you are completely satisfied with that area; in fact a 10 symbolises perfection. 10 x 10 = 100%. This allows you to work out an overall percentage figure that tells you how satisfied you are or how much further you need to go to becoming all you can be. It also identifies where you need to focus your energy. If your score is 67% and the Super You is 100% how much more can you do to get where you need to be?

Step 4: Action Plan

It is now with the left side of the brain that we need to break those goals down into measurable and achievable steps.

Break down the steps you need to take to achieve the objective.

In each of the steps write down how you are going to achieve the objective / step in detail and take accountability by saying when you will do it by.

AREA 1:

Objective	Description	Date

AREA 2:

Objective	Description	Date

AREA 3:

Objective	Description	Date

AREA 4:

Objective	Description	Date

AREA 5:

Objective	Description	Date

AREA 6:

Objective	Description	Date

So now you have broken your life down into six areas and you have a mission statement, vision, affirmations with clear goals and objectives. This has been broken down into manageable chunks to take action and work upon. For those of you who like planning then over the page there is a daily planner and weekly planner that you may find useful in organizing your life and keeping you focused on your goals. For those of you who are not as keen on such structured planning you can refer back to your overall objectives at any point.

'The world makes way for the man who knows where he is going.'
- Ralph Waldo Emerson

DAILY PLANNER
DATE

Appointments / Events	List Of Actions	Project
8am		
9am		
10am		
11am		
12pm		
1pm		
2pm		
3pm		
4pm		
5pm		

WEEKLY PLANNER
DATE

6 Key Areas	Actions	Mon	Tue	Wed	Th	Fri	Sat	Sun
		Am	Am	Am	Am	Am	Am	Am
		Pm	Pm	Pm	Pm	Pm	Pm	Pm
		Eve	Eve	Eve	Eve	Eve	Eve	Eve

To Do List

When planning it would be an idea to make your weekly/daily planner personal to yourself; perhaps you need a lot of detail or maybe you prefer a more simplistic approach. The important thing is that it helps you to focus continually on what you want to achieve. Even better, as the day, week and months go by, you get to tick off exactly what you have completed and re-focus on what you have not.

One way that this approach helped me to re-focus was when I had a bad fall playing football, twisting my pelvis and whip lashing my back. I managed to damage three vertebrae at the top and three vertebrae at the bottom. A number of people said to forget playing football again. After months of initial pain and the on set of my wheat allergy I managed to confuse the doctors as to what was wrong with me. Eventually I got to see a physiotherapist who didn't seem to work for me. I this really frustrating because I had this belief that I could play again. What kept me going was the fact I had a burning passion to play football again and I could also see the vision in my head. I also realized that I had to do everything in simple steps. I was older so my body wouldn't heal as quickly. So I went to see another physiotherapist, this time with great success. I also listened to the physio, taking everything in small steps, strengthening exercises, walking, swimming, cycling for months on end until eventually running. In fact it was hurting when I was running so I lost weight to help the load. It was then that the physiotherapist said I needed to push it. At this point, after so long in pain, I could still feel my back aching and worried it would go again. All that was left was a step of faith. We went on holiday and it was then at the family resort of the Hotel Skorpias in Cala de Or I started playing football. I have not looked back and I am playing competitive matches again and have recently picked up leading goal scorer for the season. How did this happen? They said to forget playing again! It was simple with a lot of hard work.

1. I didn't let other people put me off – it's hard enough beating your own inner demons!

2. I had a deep passion to play again.

3. I used the dreaming right side of my brain to visualize the holistic goal.

4. I consulted the best medical advice and listened to the advice.

5. I used the left side of the brain to work through a logical step by step monthly exercise plan.

6. I took action consistently with the end goal constantly in mind - playing football and scoring goals and anchoring on the feeling of scoring goals.

7. I used faith to take the first and last steps.

Here is an example of the logical left and imaginative right side of the brain working together; working in harmony to achieve the soul eventuality.

This is a good example of how planning can positively change your life.

Let's relate this all back to character and taking risks, very calculated risks perhaps, as we have considered the benefits and consequences, but it is important not to lose our spontaneity. Why is spontaneity important? Well if we plan everything in life, how exciting would that be? And sometimes you have to take risks to take part in life.

List the spontaneous things that you have done in your life that have really been special moments for you.

How good were the spontaneous things you completed and how did they make you feel? What did you learn?

Sometimes the best things in life that happen are the ones we don't plan for. If we miss the plan, so what? We can always go straight back to it. Don't feel guilty, just get back on track. Take Christmas for example. Most people decide to relax by eating and drinking whatever they want for two weeks, just like a two week holiday abroad. The simple point is, so what if we put a bit of weight on? It's simple when we get back to our plan - the weight comes back off. It's the same with anything else. Iif for a few days we can't train because we are ill or maybe we lose the whole week, so what? We get back to the plan when we are better. By having this type of attitude we are autogenically in the right frame of mind to succeed. Most people let setbacks hold them back or stop them from being all they can be. Don't.

To truly empower other people we have to trust them firstly then we have to give them opportunities to develop and grow. As an individual we have to trust in ourselves and our inner guide to empower ourselves. Empowerment is all about giving our self or other people the opportunity to build character and to build character we have to come out of the comfort zone to take risks. As we said earlier people buy people and it is possible to develop our self or other people through character building opportunities and the right attention to succeed. In so doing we are developing the cause of the soul of the company.

> *People are motivated by opportunity but afraid of change and the two go hand in hand.*

That's why a lot of people do not proactively take opportunities and a manager giving gentle encouragement to the individual is a gift as great as being the author of any book. Everybody deserves the opportunity to grow or at least try or have a go. But unfortunately closed-minded management takes us back to the industrial age where the expectation was that it is always up to the individual to find the way for themselves. When managers realize that it is their responsibility to help the people that work for them (a simple point), to empower, to coach, to lead, the world will be a better place.

What is the saying? Love thy neighbour, because we are all on the same level and we are all human. What type of world are we living in?

One of the most efficient styles of management or leadership is through the giving of special attention to show genuine interest in the colleague, because it will do the best for the individual, the organization and, in so doing, themselves. This skill in its own right will create not only an individual who acts in a greater way than the self but an organization that is united by the individual cause that is intrinsically shared by its employees as a whole.

It is finding the best road for the individual and giving all the support and help along the way.

It is also important to appreciate that within any organization that we will progress based on our dualistic tendencies. Once again the right brained of us who are not given an opportunity to express themselves will not develop as well as a left brained of us who are geared to breaking down targets, organizing a customer base, or systematically carrying out jobs of a repetitive nature. That's why it is important for individuals from the front line up to management to be measured against behaviours and key performance indicators. It is also important that we are measured in a practical as well as analytical way. It is recognizing potential in all its forms and marrying that potential to all business opportunities for all colleagues. If you were honest with yourself and listed your true potential, how it could be developed further, and where you could go or what you could be, then a potential picture can be framed that links in to your future opportunities and development. It is unselfishly in the workplace recognizing others' potential and seeking the best opportunities for those people.

Performance Review	_____	Personal Life (PL) / Appreciation of Individual
How to / Results Driven		What their motivation is internally and externally

This links in to performance management and the appraisal process. When setting performance objectives it is important to link objectives to the individual's inner motivation.

Goals	Steps	Visualization	Date	Link to PL
Objective	How to	End Result	When by	End PL goal
				i.e.
				Married
				Holiday
				Car
				Inner Reward
				Etc

It is the appreciation of the individual's inner motivation in their personal life that enables them to gain real focus for work and their work objectives. The objectives have a very focused end result in work but link these to their personal life so they visualize the holistic goal at all times – their inner purpose for working. Pictures of motivation and goals in the workplace help to continually improve the environment for positive development.

An excellent tip is to get the individual to explain the steps they have taken to achieve something in their personal life and how they have made it happen. Then, by relating that back to work and by using the same process and feelings, it shows them what is possible in the workplace.

It is said that you can't motivate anyone else, only the environment that they work in. This is basic seed theory; you plant the seed then create the right environment for the plant to grow. Believe it or not, you can't make it grow. Relating this back to humans, the supposition is that people are motivated by choice and therefore you can't motivate anyone - they can only motivate themselves. However you can set the right environmental conditions to help them motivate themselves.

Although we should get the environment right for individuals to grow and motivate themselves, there is also a definite influence one can have to motivate the individual. It is all dependent upon that individual's subconscious map of the world; their individual subterranean world of stimulus and reaction. Each person has in-built pressure points like triggers and by pressing the right trigger points it is possibly to get a reaction or response.

The premise is 'The Reactive Theory of Motivation'; that every person goes through life being motivated reactively by every single experience that takes place in their life. In fact so much so that they almost become like Pavlov's dogs in the theory of behaviourism. What happens is that we create mental models about the world from when we are young right through to adult life and develop conditioned responses to every piece of stimuli. Therefore our motivation in life is dependent upon the external stimulus we experience plus our interpretation through our past conditioning, which equals our automated instant response (as opposed to our desired response which means we stop to think and choose our response).

For example, walking down the road in the middle of summer, the whole experience of the blue sky next to the beautiful green landscape in the background can automatically motivate us – it makes you feel good. We are naturally conditioned to think it is a lovely day and hence that makes us feel good. Mental models are like subconscious triggers that automatically make us react because of the way we are programmed. How many people are miserable when the weather is poor? This is because of their subconscious triggers and the language they have been programmed to use - 'it's raining, what an awful day'...What's awful about the day? It's only raining! An example of mental models and the power of the subconscious is, have you ever started driving your car from home and then wondered how you got to your destination? You hadn't even given the road a second thought. That is because if it is a regular journey your subconscious has taken over. Is it not amazing how we can watch television, read the paper, eat our tea and talk at the same time? The point is we are programmed (to and) by our past experiences in life.

In work you are surrounded by moaners who talk negatively, which puts you in a foul mood without consciously thinking about it. We are totally reactive to most stimuli and the lazier we become or every time we make the easiest choice the more reactive we are. So if you know a person well enough you can motivate them to react without thinking things through or consciously thinking things through to get a subconscious reaction.

What I mean by that is that if I call you names you might consciously decide to hit me on the spur of the moment but afterwards regret your actions. So in this case I have motivated you enough to get you to hit me – I have created the reaction. If you had proactively been motivated the decision would have been not to take action if your beliefs were against violence. (If they were for violence then the hitting would have been proactive.)

Have you ever had a ten second drama moment in the home when someone has asked you to do something? A time when you have been completely reactive to what is probably a reasonable request?

The other side of the coin is proactive motivation where the individual through contemplation decides to act by making a conscious decision.

Cognitively the individual takes accountability but it is only proactive if they have decided to make the right decision in line with their true values.

You can motivate another person through helping them realize their goals, drives, reasons and holy grails. So that they can reactively take proactive action!

The reason man is motivated to live and can choose to be proactive is by using the will to love the self and others and to live by their values, which gives them meaning and purpose. The challenge here is to be the creating man or woman who is willing to make proactive decisions to live their life to the full. To become all that you can be by not reacting to life and carrying around so much negative energy.

When people are stressed and tired they will be even more reactive - they also find it hard to free themselves of negative energy. By choosing to be proactive you can change what you can. The following diagram builds on Covey's Circle of Influence.

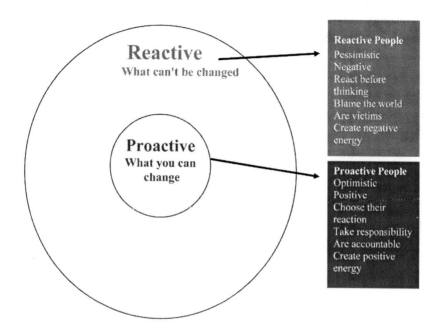

The outer circle represents the things in life that you cannot change and that is where reactive people live. They blame everything except themselves and tend to be very reactive and pessimistic in life. Reactive people tend to be negative in their outlook and react before thinking. They may feel victimized, thinking that life is beyond their control, and they create and carry negative energy around with them like baggage. This weighs them down and can have such a negative impact that it can make a person physically and mentally ill.

The inner circle is your circle of influence – this is where the proactive person lives through the freedom of their choices in life. Proactive people tend to be optimistic, positive and choose their reaction to any given situation. Proactive people generate positive energy and quickly pick themselves up after setbacks.

In any situation, it is having the ability to program yourself to think what would the Super You do? How would they react? There is the proactive answer to your life - you change what you can and live in a proactive world of positivity. You can choose who you are and what you want to be everyday.

Where the reactive father hits the child and regrets it, the proactive father takes responsibility for his actions and chooses not to react however deals with the situation in an adult manner using reason with the child. It is about changing your map of the world in the deep subconscious by reprogramming your mental models and changing your negative emotions, language and assumptions about the world, changing your beliefs and values to become truly proactive.

To be truly motivated consistently you need to be continually proactive. This is closely linked to each person's search for meaning in their life through work and how work helps them to achieve their personal goals. Relating it back to Frankl, the three ways to discover meaning are:

1. By creating a work or doing a deed.

2. By experiencing something or encountering someone (the second way of finding a meaning in life is by experiencing something – such as goodness, truth and beauty – by experiencing nature and culture or, last but not least, by experiencing another human being in his very uniqueness – by loving him).

3. By the attitude we take toward unavoidable suffering.

It is all about the realisation that you are driven by your will to love and by reprogramming yourself to realize your vast potential; to programme your self concept and self esteem. By saying yes to life and yes to yourself, realizing the Super You is possible and you can take the first steps to being continually proactive. It is then by stretching yourself physically, socially, psychologically, occupationally, and spiritually that you find meaning in life. It is having the foundation of the spirit that allows you to reach the heights of the soul through understanding your life's goals.

'What man actually needs is not a tensionless state but rather the striving and struggling for some goal worthy of him. What he needs is not the discharge of tension at any cost, but the call of a potential meaning waiting to be fulfilled by him.' - Viktor Frankl

As Frankl stresses, the meaning you associate to your 'life worth living for' becomes that innate sense of purpose and a goal of the spirit and the soul.

Fulfil your potential and realize your life's goals.

Life Changing Questions

Are you empowered at the moment and are you empowering other people?

What are your six areas of life? What is your priority?

What has the Super You achieved?

What are you willing to give to achieve your goals?

Do you live reactively or proactively?

Are you fulfilling your potential?

"Things which matter most must never be at the mercy of things which matter least." - Goethe

> *In the womb the universe began, expanding with the creation of the stars, the planets and the everlasting sun that reaches up to the heavens of the cosmos and the depths of your soul. The light bursting forth from your beginnings, the cry of life, born in to the light and in death returning to the light; vision, destiny, tale in the making.*
>
> *'Child of this Universe through spirit and soul you have become and be and become and be you will, have you stayed true to your life vision? The one set to you in birth? Your DNA and code for life. Have you consumed the fire with a passion for life and to life? To you live the dream or dream to live? What is your desire? Your need? Your ultimate motivation? I hear it calling you through the night as you search, my sweet fallen Cherubim, have you fallen from grace and in so now fallen from the path?*
>
> *If you asked your own conscience what would it say? I have set my priorities down and worked towards my life vision in line with my ideal self?*
>
> *There is still time, never to give in, never to doubt, never to late to change, to forgive, to move, to shape, to lead, to love, to give, to share, to make moments of moments, to follow your heart.'*

Summary

1. You need to empower yourself to take the first steps and continue to take action.

2. You need to have a clear life vision and broken down goals.

3. Divide your life into critical areas with mission statement, vision and affirmations – you really need to know where you are going.

4. It is about planning to make those things happen but also enjoying life's spontaneity.

5. Choose to live proactively with positive energy and optimism about your future.

6. Fulfil your true potential and work towards your dreams.

    'If one does not know to which port he is sailing, no wind is favourable.'
    - Seneca

Reality Check

Chapter 7 focuses on defining your principles and having a code for life to live by – it also discusses an example code: To Live, To Love, To Learn.

Chapter 8 looks at universal accepted truths. It focuses on your values and beliefs, and the importance of character building by taking part in life. It also focuses on the whole person character of PQ/IQ/EQ/PSYQ/SQ.

Chapter 9 breaks your life into key areas so that you set your goals with greater clarity.

In having principles, values and goals it gives you a subterranean bedrock and clear direction to work towards the Super You and the realisation of your dreams.

Interlude 3:
The Search Continues

'The way to achieve success is first to have a definite, clear practical ideal - a goal, an objective. Second, have the necessary means to achieve your ends - wisdom, money, materials, and methods. Third, adjust your means to an end.' - Aristotle

---

I
The Creating Man

See me as myself...
For I am the epitome of morning rise,
The elation of party's surprise,
The vision of kingdom comes,
The pounding of a demons drums,
The power within one life,
The cause of all worldly strife,
The passion of romance,
The hypnotiser of trance,
The guide to heavens door,
The nutshell around the core,
In time I never stray,
Yet pass by many a way.

I am the creating man,
A man apart from the many,
Thoughtful, caring, indecisive and daring,
I make with my hands the wheels of making,
I despair the death of origins undertaking,
I have love in my heart to last infinity,
And the energy of life to simple be,
I can be whatever you wish or want me to be,
For without imagination all is lost at sea.

Two opposite sides do I have to my tale,
Of right and wrong, that pass and fail,
I am loving and kind, generous and polite,
Bold, friendly, innocent, and bright,
I have so much to give, so much to share,
For a life of happiness and to want to care,
But I am also dark, strong, and taking,
Confident, illusive, a tale in the making,
A shape that spiritualises his evil ways,
Yet whose emotions run wild upon most days,
Good and evil, lost and found,
Everything and nothing, homeward bound.

I am the creating man,
That is who I am,
A wanderer, a fugitive, a king of kings,
A pauper, a player, a singer who sings.

(Usually a tune too many)

For I am the inspiration of masterpiece,
The passion that cries for universal peace,
The dedication that built Rome in a day,
The poet who has to have his say,
The stimulation towards a higher goal,
The praying man who wants a soul,
The belief to cross a dangerous land,
The fool who tries to understand,
The sailor of the deadly sea,
A passer by in history,
For life has no direct plan
In the world of the creating man.

Yet in the end there lies in my heart,
A little secret that I have kept apart,
For all of this means nothing to me
If I fail to capture the love of thee!

2

The apprentice returns from his journey -he has been gone several years on the sacred path searching for the chalice of life, the elixir of the soul, the philosopher's stone, the holy grail, the ark of the covenant - all are one and the same thing in the search forever.

He returns optimistic for the future - for though he travelled far and near his quest was not in vain as his journey had been one of character building and the apprentice was aware of the fact. His awareness had been within his aloneness, awakened, enlightened, illuminated by his own spirit to search for the end goal - his own soul.

In the question 'where lies forever?' an answer: Forever pretends to be tomorrow when really it is now, in the moment today.

'So you have returned?'

'Yes my master, I have travelled far. I have observed and I have been watching and waiting…'

'Hmmm….'

'I have learnt so much by experiencing and meeting new people, I have ventured to lands and partook in dancing rituals of different tribes. Dancing with the spirit of the lord and the thunder of her night. O how graceful was she - she the one to look upon. And I have seen oceans, valleys, mountains and brooks, glaciers, footpaths, meadows and distant shores. I have marvelled in the sunrise and gloated in the sunset. I have acknowledged every waking moment and praised the lord for my health and all my glorious senses. In that I experience all I can see, touch, hear, taste and smell. O how much I appreciate life that I am led to believe that we live in this moment to acknowledge that being alive is the appreciation of life. Every little thing I see, every texture I touch, every sound that is made in harmony with every wonderful aroma and the delicious taste of evermore life.

So here I am a man of the many.'

'What did you find?'

'*What didn't I find? I found uniqueness everywhere I went, people from different lands, all unique, gifted and special. All a sculpture of Michelangelo's David waiting to be realized, waiting in raw potential to be born.*'

'And were they ready for this?'

'*Not all my master - in fact the world is divided and mixed, diverse, and partly lost in the deep subconscious programming that is symbolic of the butterfly awaiting transformation. People are awaiting such a transformation and they are awaiting the Messiah - they are waiting for the change.*

I travelled to a land of nonchalance where the people lived by their reactions. This was a land of reactive people. Everyday they awoke and had already decided that something would spoil their day, the alarm clock, the weather, the traffic, work, their partner, money, the day before, other people, other people being richer, happier, doing well in work, better looking, in better shape…o how their negative energy drained all around.

The land of nonchalant people nobody cared - there was nothing to live for and everything to die for. Living life for the sake of it. Through the desire for pleasure or power to fill the void within their life. How you could sense the jealousy, the bitterness, the anger, the resentment, the criticized self, and the envy, the holding on to the past - the holding on to negative energy. O how this dragged each individual down as if tied like a kitten in a bag with a brick and thrown into a dark river.

I found little character of real value there. All becoming dysfunctional characters of the endless night. O what a depressing way to live but to keep oneself locked in the throws of repetitive behaviour staying within their comfort zones of the easiest choice. Never to expand or grow, bone idleness and the cheek to feel victimized by life. To blame life for their wrongs, to feel sorry for themselves, to dislike, mistrust, hate, deceive, lie, cheat, dishonour their fellow companions as well as themselves.

And what plans did they make? What dreams did they dare to dream? None.

Fallen by the wayside, too late to realize their own potential, too set in their ways. Too programmed by life to believe that it was not their fault, that they were not accountable, that they can ask life what is the meaning of life? And then be disappointed when no grand scheme is revealed.

I found myself heavy, burdened by a great sorrow and an eternal sadness that for me was so dark that I was lost in loneliness for days and weeks on end. O how I pitied the emptiness and the fear in the tragedy of their complete aloneness. No plans, no goals, complete pessimism for the future. How they would shout 'we are just being realistic and we are never let down by always expecting the worse.' How dark are their days, now and in their future present moments…lost in the past, cursing the future, conditioned by life to be reactive like a puppet on a string.

A chain reaction that has been negatively programmed into man for the last two millenniums in the teachings of the basic laws of humanity. 'Thou shall not…Thou shall not…Thou shall not…'

O how I see the parents negatively reinforcing their children with criticism, derisive comments and put downs - are these children not allowed to dream? All because the parents have lost their dreams in losing their inner child and inner character?

O how I see the teachers holding back the imagination and ideas of the children, tradition, tradition, tradition, thou shall not…

O how I see the managers brutally treat their staff no better than animals, with no trust…

And how I found myself being spiritually disconnected to everything that was graceful and pure in life. How I found no gratification in the present moment, how I was blind to the beauty of nature and our man made structures of the world, how I lost myself in the taste of forgetfulness to numb the pain through drink and narcotics lost as a shade upon the nightfall, a ghost upon the landscape.'

'And then what young apprentice?'

'I felt a force so overwhelming in a deep realization that my light was ever so close to going out, and it guided me to a distant shore where I found a new land, a new hope, a new way of life. For there my energy returned in the

surrounding glimpse of a world with delight. For I had come upon a land of caressing daylight that soothed my soul with its new found direction. Here the people moved towards a higher goal and higher self and soul.

O how charming that I could converse with such people and even disagree without even the smallest reactions. The well of life oozed from the people's willingness to take part in the moment. Never to hold on to the past and be fearful of the future. For they lived beyond the deception of time to realize now is their time. And with their time they realized that it is in their moments of decision that they shape their own destiny. For here the people only wanted to live and to live more - O how they accept each others personality types and dimensions appreciating that it is all part of being fully integrated in the amalgamation of the life cycle.

And O how fascinating they were because they were fascinated by everything in life. Life to them was a gift, something to be worshipped and cherished - they had no false Gods and religions because their God was that of life. And how they utilized every moment of breathing in a deep realization that every waking moment is enlightenment and illumination. In a deep appreciation of life they cry out for all eternity for they would wish to live for all eternity.

How this land was a waking miracle of buildings and architecture, roads and railways, land and sea, a creation to be marvelled at. O how I found myself placed before an infinite scene of beauty and O how I cried in happiness, in joy, in the feeling of being re-born.

Awakened from a bad dream!

O the parents, the teachers, the managers - all enlightened facilitators!

For here the coaching to become, to develop raw potential, to praise and encourage, to support and provide, to listen and pay attention to detail, like you my master, they are all transformational change shapers who are creating a Utopia, an Arcadia, an Avalon, a Heaven on Earth.

Thou shall they cry together, Thou shall, Thou shall.

In the freedom of their choices, a transformational world of enlightened opportunities awaiting the new Messiah.'

'You say awaiting?'

'O my master how wise you are - people in the reactive world are awaiting a Messiah. How profound and how true in the proactive world the Messiah has arrived he is with us now in our choices, in our beliefs, in our life for he is life everlasting - the soul and the spirit, for ours is the kingdom, the power and the glory forever and ever amen.'

3
A man is the sum of his choices.

Chapter 10: Personal Mastery

"You cannot teach people anything. You can only help them to discover it within themselves." - Galileo

So we now have our goals mapped out and a proactive attitude to take action. We also have gained a full understanding of and made structural changes to our principles, values and beliefs to develop character and life fulfilling experiences. So let's focus on how to keep the motivation going to consistently achieve our targets because now we know who we are, what we want and where we are going, we now have to get there. If you have travelled anywhere it actually takes some effort to get from A to B, and along the way a number of things can happen dependent upon the nature of the journey and the risk involved.

If we travel from work to home what could possibly happen? Well generally we get home without any bother, however, if we change the dynamic and say, for example, that we were travelling across the Australian outback, what could possibly happen then? We could be faced with numerous dangers and be in the grip of survival. Why is it then that a lot of people would sooner cross the outback than do a presentation or make a speech?

What is it that sometimes stops people doing the simplest of things that other people can do with ease? Why is it that some people are scared of spiders, snakes, pigeons, insects, heights, and flying for example when others are not?

Fear and it is generally an irrational fear e.g., being afraid of mice. In fact there are numerous things that could happen to us on the way home from work, but because we are conditioned to expect to get home safely we take the risk without even thinking.

Where does fear come from?

'The wall of fear is not real. It is an illusion we have been trained to treat as if it were real. This served us well in our childhood years. Our parents may have trained us to be afraid of everything new. We were much too young to know the difference between the legitimately dangerous and the merely exciting. When we grow old enough to know the difference, however, no one ever retrained us to take risks, explore new territories and treat fears as the illusions they are.

Fear is not a wall…it is a feeling, that's all. It will not (cannot) keep you from physically moving toward something unless you let it. Fear does not stop you. You stop you!' - John-Roger and Peter McWilliams

Generally fear is born from conditioning of past experience. However, irrational fear is such a deeply embedded belief that it leads to a loss or complete loss of control. This is then reinforced by our self-talk through our negative voice or voices, which become almost like demons in our head amplifying the feeling of fear.

Our self-talk is critical to our success. For example, when driving home our mind can be completely elsewhere while our subconscious mental model of how to get home takes over and gets us there. However when we are doing a presentation all of a sudden our mind can only think of what could possibly go wrong and how much of a fool we could make of ourselves. Our self-talk becomes negative therefore we become nervous, feel sick and begin to perspire. In fact sometimes we completely let our demon take over, stopping us from achieving our true potential. And who is the demon's biggest friend in life? Yes, you guessed it, the easiest choice.

For example, you have been going to the gym and you have really pushed yourself to get there, making some headway in how you look and feel. All of a sudden you get tired from work, so you skip a few but that's ok because you have been working hard. Then the demon takes over; you can't be bothered, *I don't really need to go the gym, so what if I don't look my best?* Don't listen to that voice, don't listen, but what happens? *Forget the gym, get back on the chocolate. So what?*

Our inner demon is the negative, self-doubting, dark voice that gives us feelings of insecurity when we are caught in a new situation or a past conditioned state in the present. We all have demons. The most obvious is the voice that is never happy with the way we look, the next questions our ability, the next our popularity, the next our sanity and so on. In fact it is the same negative and self-critical voice.

So how do we overcome the negative self-talk?

By using our inner coach, the higher you, or our greater subconscious, which knows the universal truths we cannot escape if we are willing to listen. It is having a conscious awareness to use positive self-talk to coach ourselves to build our self esteem through a high self-concept in line with our self-ideal – the Super You.

So let's focus on what it means to be a coach for ourselves and for other people. The coach is the '*who*' helps you get there and through their expertise they help you with the '*what*' and the '*how*' and '*when*' you are going to get there.

Before we focus on your inner coach, let's focus on what coaching is first.

What is coaching?

A means for learning.
Helping someone achieve his or her goals.
Facilitating positive change.
A coach asking questions to develop the coachee.
The coach developing understanding and accountability in the coachee.
Step change development.
Inspiring and supporting another person.
Performance and behavioural output improvement.

Why Coach?

There are numerous reasons why it is important to provide quality coaching to other people in life and in the workplace, and with ourselves through our own self-talk.

> To motivate and inspire yourself or others
> To pass on experience
> To develop yourself or another individual
> To unlock potential
> To value yourself or another person by listening
> To gain or give them individual realization
> To develop understanding and accountability
> To produce a winning formula or team
> To enhance performance
> To really make a difference in your own life and in others
> To provide special attention
> To instil belief in yourself or another

We all act as coaches at some point in our life, whether that be coaching our children to read or helping them with homework, to taking a more active role in work or perhaps with a hobby or sport. Choosing to be a coach is a way of life and it is important to realize that through our own inner voice and self-talk that we coach ourselves everyday.

Coaching is the art of changing behaviour in a positive way to help the individual or ourselves realize their full potential.

So how do we inner coach ourselves? By using the same techniques and principles used to coach others to coach ourselves. If only we were to listen to the voices in our head then, dependent upon the mood we are in, will depend upon the outcome in behaviour at a particular time. Dependent upon the mood we are in there will also be an association to our past experience hence triggering through our mental models a natural reactive response. This is so similar to the level of flight or fight response back in our caveman days, an instant response without thinking. The easiest choice in this case is to be driven by our mood, which dictates our response and generally less work. The opposite can also be the case where we actually over think through endless possibilities with the mindless chattering of thoughts running through our head.

You become what you think about the most.

If our mind is continually dwelling on issues then not only are we wasting energy but we are also re-enforcing the situation. It also means there will be a lack of action caused by hesitation of our fear. So what are the reasons that cause us to doubt or fear or lack confidence?

- A feeling of incompetence in a given activity or skill – a lack of self-confidence

- A hard or unpleasant task – leads to procrastination through an internal belief

- Past Experience – external conditioning leads to negative belief

- Mood – how you are feeling e.g. you are not in the right frame of mind

- Opinion – self-conditioning negative belief

- Imagination – painting worst case scenario pictures in your mind

So how do we overcome the feeling of fear? Some would advise us to face our fears to prove it is mind over matter.

Fear is a state of mind re-enforced by our inner critical demon/voice chattering away endlessly. To be able to overcome our demons our self-talk is critical and it is via our inner coach that personal mastery becomes possible.

Personal mastery is the ability to control your emotional state and reactions.

Our inner coach chooses our reaction through a calm state of mind choosing not to be influenced by past experience or existing emotion.

It is an assertive calmness that thinks before choosing the action in line with our values.

Stimuli → Inner Coach Considers → Chosen response

> *Personal mastery is the ability to work towards goals the benefit of which provides leverage to maintain motivation.*

Your inner coach chooses character and competence building goals that stretch you to work towards the Super You.

> *Personal mastery is the art of being a change facilitator, which is the ability to question and listen to yourself to promote positive change.*

The main skills of the coach are to question the coachee to explore their situation so both the coach and the coachee gain understanding. Empathetic listening makes the coachee feel valued as the coach builds on the coachee's answers. The coach then facilitates the coachee to take accountability by designing an action plan of 'what' the coachee is going to do to improve performance, 'how' they are going to do it and by 'when', gaining full commitment from the coachee to determine their will to make it happen.

We coach ourselves exactly the same way by exploring how we feel about the goal and then developing an action plan that we are committed to work towards. It is also about being connected with ourselves on a deep empathetic level.

Generally we have an idea about what we want but when do we really question and listen to ourselves?

> *Personal mastery is having the willpower to make positive changes by taking action.*

The ability and determination to make changes, especially structural changes, to our beliefs and then continue to take action, living by the changes we have made, takes willpower; the willingness to make those changes consistently and work them through to the end.

> *Personal mastery is about integrity, honour and truth.*

To live by our code and in saying yes to our self one can be true to oneself. It is by honouring our code and taking action with integrity that we hold true to our self. The Super You has a clear conscience and through that it is possible to be our self – merely natural. To be able to coach our self we need to eliminate negative talk and destructive thoughts. There are several techniques that the inner coach can use to programme the mind.

> *'If you really want to improve your outer world, whether this means your health, your relationships or your finances, you must first improve your inner world. The most effective way to do this is through the practice of continuous improvement. Self mastery is the DNA of life mastery.' - Robin Sharma - The Monk Who Sold His Ferrari*

Overcoming Demons

How aware are you of your inner demons? What do you fear? What do you doubt yourself in? What do you lack confidence in?

List your fears   Why is it a fear? (Keep asking 'why?')

F - Future E - Expectations of A - Anticipated R - Reality

It is important to establish the real why or deep beliefs we have that may be holding us back. In analysing why the belief exists will be the core to us changing and living free from our demons i.e.

I'm afraid of flying.

Why?

I'm scared of heights.

Why?

I'm scared of falling.

Why?

I'm scared of dying.

Why?

I don't want to lose my family.

Why?

Because I love them so much I don't want to be without them.

Why?

Because I can't handle it - it makes me sick.

Generally using this technique will highlight that we can't handle the feeling of our fear or it is a feeling of insecurity in not being good enough.

'When you control your thoughts, you control your mind. When you control your mind, you control your life. And once you reach the stage of being in total control of your life, you become the master of your destiny.'

Robin Sharma - The Monk Who Sold His Ferrari

Letting Go

Yoda: *Premonitions, premonitions. Hmmmm, these visions you have...*

Anakin: *They are of pain, suffering, death...*

Yoda: *Yourself you speak of, or someone you know?*

Anakin: *Someone...*

Yoda: *Close to you?*

Anakin: *Yes.*

Yoda: *Careful you must be when sensing the future, Anakin. The fear of loss is a path to the dark side.*

Anakin: *I won't let these visions come true, Master Yoda.*

Yoda: *Death is a natural part of life. Rejoice for those around you who transform into the Force. Mourn them, do not. Miss them, do not. Attachment leads to jealousy. The shadow of greed, that is.*

Anakin: *What must I do, Master Yoda?*

Yoda: *Train yourself to let go of everything you fear to lose.*

In this case no matter how much we love someone we have to go with the natural cycle of life – certain things will happen in life that we have no control over so why worry about what we can't change? Once again it is another form of negative energy that is wasted energy through the worry of endless possibilities that may never happen. So, instead of living in a reactive world holding on to fear (negative energy), free yourself. In the above example love our family whole-heartedly but don't dwell on eventualities that may never happen.

Life has a soul's cause and a soul's eventuality – don't live in fear and bondage to a tomorrow that may never happen.

Procrastination

A lot of people put things off out of fear of potential consequences or through the thought of the task being hard work and taking up too much energy. So how do we coach ourselves to take action?

If we explore all the reasons why we are putting off the task, i.e. going to the gym, packing in smoking, decorating the bedroom, clearing out the attic, and so on that we gain full understanding of our situation. Then we can explore the consequences of taking no action and comparing these to the benefits of making the change, concluding with an action plan that secures our commitment to take action as soon as possible.

Coaching yourself through the Aspiration & Achievement Model

This model can be applied to our work or personal goals. It is a simple six step process that enables our inner coach to identify the goal and then gain understanding of our situation. Through the experience, we gain an understanding of our own situation, which leads to enlightenment, which in turn leads to aspiration. The inner coach then empowers us to take accountability for our own actions, which leads to achievement.

Step 1 Self Rapport

The inner coach sets the scene, and builds general rapport by discussing how you are feeling and how things are going. Then it identifies the objective and end goal of the coaching session.

Step 2 Explore the Goal

You now ask questions to explore the goal, picking up on all angles.

The aim is to go in depth about the goal and the inner coach asks questions and listens. (The key word here is 'explore' as a coach should not guide the individual straight to the action plan.) So it is about writing down everything about your objective and what is presently happening.

Step 3 Identify the Consequences

Identify the consequences of not achieving the goal and list them. This is to assimilate any pain attached to what the worst-case scenario would be.

Step 4 Discuss the Benefits

Identify the benefits of achieving the goal. The benefits should then be compared to the consequences.

Step 5 Accountability

Take accountability for the goal by defining an action plan. Identify 'what the next steps are', 'how you are going to do it', and 'when you will do it by'.

Step 6 Action

This last step is to discuss what the results will be and consider who can support you.

If we apply these steps to our life then any task we are procrastinating about can quickly be achieved. It is the taking accountability for our own actions that makes the difference.

Personal mastery is about understanding ourselves.

By understanding ourselves through contemplation and asking the right questions, our ability to remain focused enables us to conquer our inner critical demons. The inner coach realizes that each new day is an opportunity to become all we can be, and makes the most of the present moment by having the perfect day.

We are unique, special, intelligent and a character of purpose working towards our life's goals. It is understanding our purpose that enables our inner coach to draw upon the vision, principles, values, beliefs, and code that we set.

It is through raising self awareness that we start to understand the self, how our brain operates in a logical or creative way, our learning style, what motivates us, and how we make decisions, that enables our inner coach to challenge the inner demons in being true to our self.

> *'If you had a friend who talked to you like you talked to you, would he or she still be a friend, or would he or she be a friend for very long?' - Anon*

It is through positively affirming ourselves and by choosing how to respond that we develop personal mastery.

> *Personal mastery requires mental toughness.*

This is about having the mental toughness to apply self-discipline to our self-talk and to our internal pictures of ourselves. How we see our self is critical to our success and it is realising we can choose the landscape and meaning of every experience within our own mind.

It is the ability to deal with setbacks as challenges and never give up on our goals. Some hesitate because of fear of failure but failure is only a condition of the mind, where some fail others realize it is just not the right way to success but that it is a useful lesson a long the way. Generally it is the inner game of wills of the inner coach and demon. Those of us who have mental toughness prioritise our goals and can deal with setbacks. We handle the not so nice stuff to do and normally do it first. Where some of us put off what we don't like doing, an assertive person will do it first and then enjoy the rest of the day. The concept is one of delaying gratification i.e. eating what you don't like first and saving the best until last – how many people do this the other way around especially when they are hungry?

Realising that thinking something is not easy or nice to do is a condition of the mind. How many times have we put off making a phone call that once eventually made, is never really that bad an experience?

Life is our tale in the making – it is what you are living right now.

If when you died you were sat before God and he asked you to tell the tale of your life, how would you tell it? Like it happened to you or that you took part and made decisions about the direction along the way? Would you be proud to tell your tale or ashamed at your lack of achievement?

In any situation we can choose who we want to be, any character at any time, we can choose to be a character at the right moment for the right situation. We can write our own script – it's whether we can really be bothered making the effort to make the choices that lead to standing out from the crowd.

Modelling others' success or playing the part of a fictional character can help us become, feel and be more. Alexander the Great carried a copy of the Iliad everywhere he went, using Achilles as his role model whilst he conquered most of the ancient world. Most of us subconsciously copy our heroes and heroines without thinking – we can actually choose to be Indiana Jones in our own style at the next work meeting, we can stand up for ourselves and others like Gandhi or feel the force like Luke Skywalker. The choice is ours as to who we model our self upon, and we can model excellent behaviour to become our personal best.

With every experience we encounter we can choose who we are being, how we react and exactly what it means.

> *Life has no meaning except the one you give it and nothing in life has any meaning other than the one you choose.*

It is understanding that life, through the history of mankind, and conditioning through each and every experience in our life, is in part an illusion. Creative avoidance becomes the vice for most in following the conditioned programme to conform, to remain in the comfort zone and to take the easiest choice. Meaning becomes meaning only when we take ownership and accountability to work with our meaning, to work towards our cause and inner purpose.

Continually asking ourselves what will make the biggest difference to my life right now and doing something about it.

The will to become cries out to be fulfilled – the essence of being is glorified by the release from all fears.

To be free of the mindless chattering, to be in control and have no control,

Completeness and emptiness,

Essence and Realm.

> *"The greatest danger for most of us is not that our aim is too high and we miss it, but that it is too low and we reach it." – Michelangelo*

COACHING IS A WAY OF LIFE - TRANSFORM YOUR OWN LIFE!

Life Changing Questions

Which voice do you listen to the most?

What are your inner demons?

How can you overcome those demons?

What is your relationship like with yourself and those you coach?

What models/techniques can you use to facilitate a positive change?

Who can you successfully coach to improve your life?

Who can coach you?

Who can you ask questions and listen to?

What questions can you ask yourself to make a big difference in your life?

What 3 actions could make the biggest difference to your life right now?

How could you put those actions into place and by when?

> *'If we value independence, if we are disturbed by the growing conformity of knowledge, of values, of attitudes, which our present system induces, then we may wish to set up conditions of learning which make for uniqueness, for self-direction, and for self-initiated learning.' – Carl Rogers*

> 'And so upon the land man and woman made their mark through civilization, creating buildings, towers, settlements and cities. Raging war and destruction upon this beautiful Earth and in contrast creating sculpture, art, philosophy and religion. Generations walked the Earth asking the same unanswered questions yet all came to suffer the same fate. For all looked within the waters or mirrors of reflection to see their own face and what do they still see - Fear. Fear of themselves in their dark and their light, fear of their choices and their consequences, fear from their past and in their future. Let me ask you what do you fear? Why do you fear? Is it your light or your darkness? What fear can there be when you are true to yourself my bringer of life? For my child the soul's cause and soul's eventuality will happen anyway - why be in fear?'

Summary

1. It is fear and your inner demon (critical self doubting voice) that stops you becoming the Super You - it works with the easiest choice.

2. To overcome your demons use positive self-talk through inner coaching.

3. Coaching is the art of changing behaviour in a positive way to help the individual realize their full potential.

4. The skills of the inner coach are the ability to ask questions and listen.

5. Personal mastery is the ability to control your emotional state and reactions.

6. Personal mastery is the ability to work towards goals, the benefit of which provides leverage to maintain motivation.

7. Personal mastery is the art of being a change facilitator, which is the ability to question and listen to yourself to promote positive change.

8. Personal mastery is having the willpower to make positive changes by taking action.

9. Personal mastery is about integrity, honour, and truth.

10. Personal mastery is understanding yourself and requires mental toughness.

11. Life has no meaning except the one you give it and nothing in life has any meaning other than the one you choose.

12. Coaching is a way of life.

'First say to yourself what you would be; and then do what you have to do.' - Epictetus

Chapter 11: Characterisation - The Process of Becoming

"To improve is to change, to be perfect is to change often."
– Winston Churchill

We have looked at coaching ourselves through our inner voice; the inner voice that develops character through the freedom and wisdom of our choices. The process of becoming exists when we work toward a fixed goal or goals, it is the process of turning into something, it is the moving with change and ultimately it is through learning by experience the development of the self to become all we can be. To understand the process of becoming it is important to have an understanding of the 3 You's. There is the 'Real You', the person you really are right now and believe yourself to be; there is the 'Super You' which is your ideal self, the 'you' that you were meant to be; and there is also the 'Blind You' which is how others perceive you and that which you do not know about the self. So it is the 'you' others know.

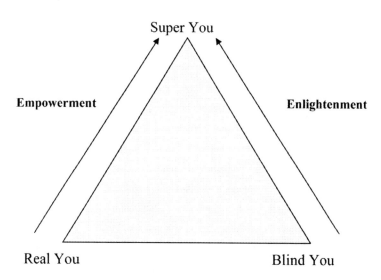

The goal of becoming is the Super You, the 'you' you were meant to be, and to get there from the Real You we have to empower ourselves to take action and risks. From the Blind You we have to enlighten ourselves by actively seeking feedback and self-analysing our performance and behaviour.

The process of becoming is a model of development that can be applied at any level of work or to any interest we have as the process of development is the same. Development is through a hierarchical framework, which for our motivation and becoming is essential - it is the development of character and competence.

New Skill / New Role/ New Interest

When starting any new task the initial development phase is one of aspiration, the aspiration to achieve the goal, to be skilled in a given task, to reach out for the dream. The aspirational level is the goal setting stage where we start with a greater vision of where we would like to go or what we would like to become. It is then the breaking down of immediate goals to learn the basics. Once we have passed through the aspirational phase we then continue towards the end goal by performing at a consistent level which requires continual motivation. To reach out to the next level we have to live in a motivational way to acquire the necessary skills or steps to reach the talented inspirational level. The inspirational level is that of the master, the professional, the inspirational change facilitator.

To inspire is to aspire and to aspire is to inspire.

Take a coach or trainer for example - when the coach starts they may have in mind the aspiration of becoming a great coach or trainer and it is that aspiration that needs to be nurtured once they have become competent at the basics and they are displaying the will to progress to the next level of expectation. It becomes one of motivational high expectation. You expect them to be motivated to achieve the next steps and also that each time they coached or trained that they would be of a motivational standard. The length of time spent at this level is dependent upon the skill, desire and potential of the individual to progress. Once they become the expert coach or trainer in the way they work, behave and act then they progress to the next level, that of the inspirational coach or trainer. To inspire is to create aspiration in others and aspiration will eventually lead to inspiration through hard work, dedication and motivation.

The process of becoming works through these stages in the development of character and competence. Let's focus on competence first.

Competence

In the workplace it is essential to have competent employees who can complete a task effectively or service a customer properly; having competent staff cuts down on the risk factors that most industries are now scrutinised upon. To develop competence the individual receives training and is observed and assessed in the required tasks to be signed off as competent. Development solutions specifically tailored to the role, along with quality leadership and coaching are required. Competence is the development of the knowledge and skills to be able to complete the given task or role effectively. You develop the way, ability or capability to a competent standard.

Character

Character is the development of attitude and behaviour. In any role when you advance in your career one's level of responsibility increases and with that so do desired expectations of behaviour. There is a certain code of conduct that is expected at each level. Most people naturally adjust their attitude and behaviour to mirror their level of responsibility to the point that some people alienate themselves by going too far, completely changing and losing friends.

How do we develop character? As mentioned earlier, character is based on our experiences and how we learn from those experiences. It is also deeply linked to our values and hence our shared values when it comes to an employer. We develop character through our choices and our willingness to take up new challenges and to raise our expectations. It is the ability to choose our attitude in any situation and can be measured by our will or willingness.

Moving through the phases at an aspirational level we would expect a burning desire to take up the new challenge and a willingness to learn and be developed. At a motivational level the willingness is one of accountability and responsibility to consistently perform to motivate others. At an inspirational level we lead by example and inspire through living as role models.

We develop character in life by modelling others from growing up as a child copying parents, to copying friends growing up, to watching films and copying our heroes or heroines, to copying in work, hobbies, interests.

We aspire to be like someone else and in doing so we completely model ourselves in line with our vision of what we believe good or cool to look like. Therefore all external stimuli that we associate with, and give meaning to, motivate us. We are continually moving towards or moving away from stimuli in line with a greatest value - the vision of what we want ourselves to be.

226

It is essential to have a strong picture of the Super You so that everything we associate with is in line with everything we want to be. Therefore we will be motivated to move towards our goal and the subconscious will model our character to the desired vision.

This is 'Characterization', the modelling of all the desired characteristics of external stimuli i.e. people we aspire to be like, and within that, the process of becoming to become all we can be. Unfortunately the picture we hold sometimes can be completely dysfunctional. For example, we are programmed to think by certain stimuli that it is cool to be the bad guy.

So what can we do to programme ourselves to subconsciously move towards the Super You? There are a number of techniques, some of which we have already discussed, that can be developed through our inner coach.

Visualisation

Visualising the Super You and then moving towards that vision or visualising the success of something we intend to do and then doing it. When in doubt, we ask ourselves what the Super You would do in this situation.

Anchoring

This is remembering a past experience where we felt fantastic or great, e.g., completing an achievement, or at a particular time, or a previous feeling. We then re-create that feeling by visualizing it and feeling the same feelings we felt back then now hence changing our state. We then attach an anchor to the state e.g. clenching our fists or touching our ear. When we touch our ear in the future it helps us to re-create the desired state. Alternatively we may say something that creates the state.

Subliminal Affirmations

By saying positive affirmations in our mind over and over again with concentrated attention, the idea repeated will tend to spontaneously realize itself. This is because the affirmations are tapping directly into the subconscious mind, which is subliminal reinforcement through repetition and the affirmations being spoken in the present tense.

Modelling

This is literally copying the desired traits of others that we want to develop within ourselves, e.g. copying a famous character in a film, or a famous sports star. Growing up, we all had heroes and heroines that we wanted to be like and then we would pretend to be like. If we want the perfect relationship, then we find someone with that relationship and ask him or her just what it is that makes it perfect and then model our relationship upon that. If we want to be good at a job we find someone who excels at that job and then ask him or her why he or she excels, what do they do, and then we model their behaviour.

If we want to be the best we have to be like the best or as someone once said 'I don't want to be the best, I want to be better.'

Association

Association is taking an existing undesired habit and breaking the habit by associating the worst of consequences of continuing the habit and programming that deeply in the mind. We can re-condition ourselves with the new habit and associate all the benefits and the feelings those benefits will create. By programming our self for a 30-day period to continually form the new habit through conditioning will deeply embed the change and that change is more likely to stick, therefore resulting in living by the new and desired habit of behaviour.

State Changing

This is literally changing state by altering our physiology. For example if we are feeling depressed then we can smile and laugh, which will change state and start to make us feel good. To state change we can model others' physiology to get the desired results.

Energy Generator

This is literally all about creating energy - getting up and doing something - which is great coupled with a stated anchor e.g. 'work hard', 'live strong' etc Just by clapping our hands vigorously, we can change our state.

Autogenic Conditioning

The word autogenic means self origin so autogenic conditioning is conditioning from oneself. The concept was devised by Johannes Schultz in the 1930's and quite simply the concept is that the body follows the dictates of the mind. Therefore we can put our self in a relaxed state of mind, which then influences our body. Here the placebo effect means that people who strongly believe in a remedy for example tend to get better. After Schultz invented the technique German athletes used it to enhance their performance. This had significant effect, increasing the ability of the athletes through relaxed visual techniques. In the 1940's/50's German athletes dominated the Olympic Games and the secret to their success was autogenic conditioning. It is proven that negative thoughts and emotions have negative effect on our muscles while positive thoughts will have a positive effect.

There are two ways to condition the mind to have ultimate effect:

1. To use relaxation techniques along with visualization to create the Super You achieving your goals. In a relaxed state our subconscious is more open to persuasion and by programming the subconscious this way it presumes the visualization is reality - this is then reinforced with subliminal affirmations.

2. To be able to reach a tranquil state no matter what happens. For example you are playing Tennis and you have lost the first set and you are not playing as well as you would like. Instead of allowing it to affect you, you stay in a completely relaxed state with a deep inner belief that you will win (similar to letting go of fear in the last chapter).

What does the ability to apply all these techniques rely upon?

Our inner voice and inner character and more importantly our self talk through our inner coach.

As stated in the previous chapter we are our own coach through our inner voice and the way we talk to ourselves. The way we talk to our self is based on the Real You and who we really believe our self to be - the current us. It is through what we think about our self, our self-concept and what we really feel about our self, (our self-esteem) which our beliefs about our self are based upon. There is also the Blind You and through seeking feedback from other people we can generate a greater awareness of the Real You.

We have already assessed what you want out of life; the focus now is how to get there. It is about having the will and finding the way in life that empowers people to succeed. In essence...

The will to love and the way to life!

So if our aim is to be all that we can be and to become truly inspirational people, what is inspirational? How many inspirational people have you met in your life? What made them inspirational?

Well I would guess that any inspirational person you have met has been either credible because they are more than competent in capability and that they have higher character. But what is it that makes them inspirational?

* They have reached a great achievement you admire?
* They have suffered a great tragedy and survived to tell the tale?
* They have achieved the impossible?
* They have expert knowledge?
* They have self-belief and instil belief in others?
* They can capture an audience with their experiences and stories?
* They have innate direction and belief in cause?
* They have a rich and warm enigmatic personality?
* They have the ability to build relationships with all levels of people?
* They transform people's lives?
* They lead by example and people willingly follow with conviction?
* They create a motivational environment and make life interesting?
* They challenge the status quo to constantly improve the world?
* They always go the extra mile?
* They constantly move out of their comfort zone taking people with them?

The above are just some questions and measures of inspiration. How many inspirational people have you met and how memorable are they?

In becoming everything we can be, to be truly inspirational takes an awful lot of determination and courage. It is the great desire to become all we can be and fulfil our destiny.

The inspirational master lives their dream. Being totally true to themselves with a deep understanding of why they are here, and living in total harmony with their vision and purpose.

To be inspirational is a chosen way of life which is the Super You.

In returning to the Super You - in what way is the Super You inspirational?

What will you do to go the extra mile and take your level of performance +1?

We need aspirations and the greater the vision, the greater we feel, the greater we model excellent behaviour, in a proactive world, we can all truly become the best we can.

> *How can you inspire yourself, the people you love, the people you work with, and the world?*

The next chapter explores the main source of the will to love and inspiration.

Life Changing Questions

Who is the real you?
How can you empower yourself?
How can you enlighten the blind you?
How are you developing competence?
How are you developing character?
What are you aspiring to be?
What and how are you presently motivational?
What are you inspirational in?
How are you inspirational?
How can you become inspirational?
How can you inspire the world?

> *'I have learned, that if one advances confidently in the direction of his dreams, and endeavours to live the life he has imagined, he will meet with a success unexpected in common hours.' - Henry David Thoreau*

'What was this dream? Excelsior! Thee thy divine child sent to Earth without wings, born with a greater destiny and purpose. Born in to the light to bring light, to shape life and live life. Where have you gone my Excelsior? I see your intention but I see no action, I feel your hearts content and can touch your dreams but only sorrow and shortcomings have become your becoming. O child can you not see your right to be inspirational, to shine forth unto this world, a soul bringer, a life bringer, a rule maker and a shape changer. Do you not see your choices on the roads to Galilee? Free to choose, born free to live, or free to die? How I cry for the Super You to come forth within this the Essence and the Realm of your life. For what is this heavenly host for you to live like a ghost upon the landscape?'

Summary

1. The goal of becoming is the Super You and to get there from the Real You we have to empower our self to take action. From the Blind You we have to enlighten our self by actively seeking feedback and self-analyzing our performance and behaviour.

2. To inspire is to aspire and to aspire is to inspire.

3. To become we work through 3 levels of character and competence building, the aspirational, the motivational and inspirational.

4. Characterization is the modelling of all the desired characteristics of external stimuli i.e. people we aspire to be like and within that the process of becoming to become all we can be.

5. It is about having the will and finding the way in life that empowers people to succeed. In essence the will to love and the way to life!

6. How can you be inspirational in life and go +1?

   "The truth of the matter is that there's nothing you can't accomplish if: (1) You clearly decide what it is that you're absolutely committed to achieving, (2) You're willing to take massive action, (3) You notice what's working or not, and (4) You continue to change your approach until you achieve what you want, using whatever life gives you along the way." - Anthony Robbins

Chapter 12: Special Attention

"Any fool can make things bigger, more complex, and more violent. It takes a touch of genius and a lot of courage to move in the opposite direction." - Albert Einstein

In 1859 Charles Darwin published a book so heretical it literally challenged every single person's view of the world. The Origin of the Species was beautifully written and completely radical, and completely on a par with Galileo's claim that the Earth was round - a complete paradigm shift that stunned the human race. Darwin had confided to a friend that it was 'like confessing a murder'.

Evolution – dictionary definition:

A process of change in a particular direction; the process by which something attains its distinctive characteristics; a theory that existing types of plants and animals have developed from earlier forms.

Evolve – dictionary definition:

To unfold; to open out; to develop.

The concept of Evolution is that every living species evolves through a process of natural selection. The simplicity and elegance of natural selection explains that through evolution the journey of life becomes a test of survival: ***the survival of the fittest to adapt to their particular surroundings.*** These surroundings can be the existing climate that provides the challenge of self-preservation each day or a new environment that provides the opportunity of colonisation. Evolution's aim is to become the fittest within the chain therefore prolonging survival and endurance. The downside to survival is not only death, but also extinction of the species.

Relating that to human development we evolve as deep spiritual beings through the will to love. Natural selection is the process of becoming all that we can be; selecting to evolve through our own choice to face life's challenges.

How true this is in relation to the present work climate and the competition of businesses and organizations - only the fittest through profit survive. Our aim as an employee may be to evolve to become the best we possibly can be, to the point we want to become the best in our particular chain/department or to produce quality work to perpetuate. Our fear of extinction is not just to be pushed slowly through the door through poor performance or redundancy, but that our work is forgotten and has counted for nothing. Is it that in general man wants to feel that his existence counts within the organization and that his sense of self worth is echoed if his existence is valued?

This is mankind's will to self-evolution - that this life counts for something.

Frankl explains that mankind's main source of motivation is the will to meaning and through lack of meaning in life the result will be an existential vacuum. He also explains that the will to pleasure (Freud) and will to power (Adler / Nietzsche) are compensation for a lack of meaning. Therefore many individuals will spend their life pursuing pleasure or power, even to the point of addiction, to fill the vacuum of no meaning in their life. Regardless the extent of attainment of power or pleasure many find that the vacuum needs to be continually filled only to find that the void is never satisfied without meaning or purpose of the universal kind.

Having meaning in our life is essential in living a healthy life however the real driving force to survival, pleasure, power, and meaning is the will to self love and self evolution. The search for this meaning is done through special attention applied through self-love.

Special attention is the action of the will to love and the end product.

It is the appreciation of the self through love that drives one to desire meaning for our existence. If we do not value our self then we will not go in search of meaning or be driven by the will to meaning. One might say that through lack of meaning there is no self-value which, without love of the self in the first place, no will to meaning will completely fill that existential vacuum. Love as a dual driving force is a marriage of the opposites because through love can meaning be found both on an inner and outer level. Meaning can be found with the self or through another person/s.

Love is all.

Maslow's 'Hierarchy of Needs' which is based on the concept that individuals require satisfaction on ascending levels of need is driven by the will to love. It is through love of the self that we seek physiological, security, social, esteem and actualization needs and their satisfaction.

All our indirect wills are a by product of the will to love, the will to survive, the will to maintain survival, the will to reproduce/pleasure/acceptance, the will to power and the will to meaning. Through meaning there is definitely reason to live but it is through love that we find that meaning.

> *Giving special attention through the will to love leads to a positive outcome.*

How many examples can you think of where you have received special attention or have given attention? If you have ever been married, how does it feel to receive all that special attention leading up to the wedding and on the day itself? Amazing. Can you imagine how it would be if people showed one another that attention all of the time. Can you imagine feeling that good all of the time? My question is why don't we do this all the time?

Leadership is all about having the ability to give the right attention at the right time to inspire and create; yet how often do managers concentrate on figures and task at the expense of their people? It is the attention alone that creates the change in behaviour and if that attention is credible and genuine then that change is multiplied to produce outstanding results.

In an example of providing the right attention, when I was working for one of the main UK banks, we provided an Operational Training Programme which offered a portfolio of courses for Customer Service and Sales Agents. These courses offered the individual the promise of learning new ideas and skills as well as the motivation and confidence to transfer the skills to have big impact back in the workplace. The challenge was to give experienced staff credible sales and service training that made a difference. As part of the evaluation the Operational Training Programme results illustrated the following: -

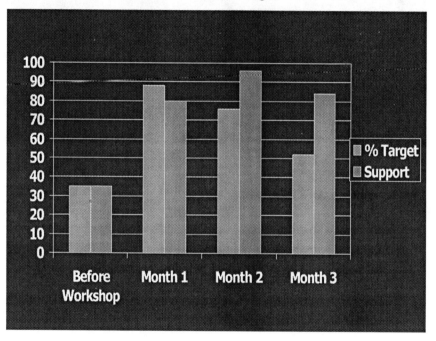

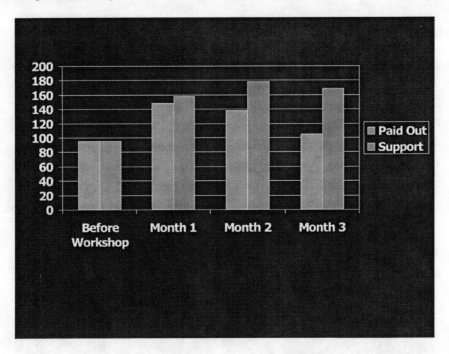

Performance and Business

1. There was a large improvement in individual performance and business impact through paid out business (Illustrated % to target of the population in graph 1 and paid out business in graph 2).

2. The overall results showed that impact was greatest in the first month after training and then trailed off.

3. Those individuals that received relevant follow up support from the action planning process continued to improve and maintain performance.

The results highlighted that there is immediate impact straight after the course. This can be linked to the Hawthorne Effect, which showed that if an experimental group is given special attention the individual and group produce much better results. Sometimes the individual learns a great deal during the course and at other times they may just be completely refreshed with a renewed vigour that provides the motivation to improve their performance. One thing that is definite is if the individual feels or has felt the course has been beneficial and motivational then the special attention they have received will make a difference. So the attention they receive has to be credible.

When the individual received relevant support and attention from the coach (line manager) after the course/s the results were quite staggering, almost doubling the performance results of individuals. This led to the following equation.

Special Attention = Improved Performance and Motivation

The special attention received needs to be credible and proactive to make a difference - this is a business illustration for how special attention can make that difference. However even without the evidence one could say that it is good common sense to know that if we give someone special attention that is credible then they will be motivated or even inspired to make positive changes. Another consideration should be the timing of the attention. This can be illustrated through the **Motivational Attention Spiral.**

The **Motivational Attention Spiral** is a theory that suggests that during a learning event or training average human concentration spans are 20 minutes. That is why it is important to change exercises, subjects, approach to energise and create positive energy. Each time concentration drops new motivational material needs to be introduced to maintain levels of interest, energy and vitality. Hence a good facilitator will use high energy exercises and energizers to make the learning event an entertaining and pleasurable experience to make sure that transfer of learning takes place. This is essential in all our relationships if we want to be successful in life. We should think of all the different ways we can apply attention and create energy. Most relationships fail because of boredom or differences or having nothing in common. To make relationships work you have to be willing through the will to love to apply attention, work hard and create an environment of energy and interest. Special attention is the most effective tool to make our life work on an individual level, with other people and to evolve.

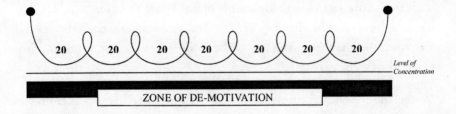

Applying it to our personal life will depend on each person...what is important here is the need to provide special attention within our life for our self. As already mentioned the existential vacuum claims many of us when we forget to provide meaning or attention in our life. When this is applied to managing or leading a team the gap between spirals may be larger although the principle is the same. We should consider how we could get our team to use special attention within the team and towards one another to create a highly energetic team environment and spirit.

From an employer's point of view it is not only important to understand that the need for special attention needs to be applied to the employee but that it is also needed when one thinks the individual needs it the least. It is not always obvious that the individual is on a downward spiral especially as each individual's spiral time will differ and everyone needs attention.

> *The key to success in your life is to use the energy of your will to love and to apply special attention to your own life and others.*

The will to love's power is in the evolution of the human spirit in giving of the self and love.

Special attention as a tool can be applied in many ways: -

Applied to the self: Looking after the self psychologically, physically, mentally, emotionally and spiritually. It is applying attention to the detail of looking after our health and well being, to learning to expand the mind, praising and rewarding the self, positive self-talk, building effective relationships, giving love to the self and having a deeper appreciation for one's own uniqueness and unique talents.

Applied to your Family: Giving love - not reacting, being thoughtful - not shouting, but praising - not put downs or moaning, but working together towards shared family values and goals.

Applied to other people: Instead of being reactive our proactive giving of love to others through genuine special attention to detail making others feel good about themselves.

Applied to work: Leading by example and giving more than anyone else - developing and helping others; reward and recognition, compliments and praise.

Applied to life: Common courtesy and manners, being friendly at all times, living by our principles and values, saying yes to life, being optimistic, living proactively, wanting the best for others as well as ourselves.

Applied to home: Paying attention to the details of our home to have nice surroundings which are personal. Building a home of spiritual and family strength which gives us the platform, or foundation, of our own inner strength.

> *Special attention creates positive energy through the will to love thyself, others and life.*

We are all human and we all make mistakes so have you ever at home lost your temper or shouted at loved ones maybe because we were tired or we had a bad day at work? In fact have you ever had a 10 second drama when someone has asked you to do something at home and you complained like a child? Yes, it happens all the time, especially when we choose to live reactively. There are a lot of people who use positive energy all day in work, giving special attention to a lot of people who, in the bigger picture or scheme of things, are not as important as their family. Then they go home and react negatively to every situation, shouting at or smacking the kids, arguing with their partner physically or mentally, neglecting the home and so on. The freedom to choose a positive response and create a reinforced positive environment that will be conducive to growth and happiness depends on using special attention with the people who matter the most.

If you go home and actually tell your wife or husband how beautiful they are and how much you appreciate them, how does that make them feel? Yet how often do we do it? In fact how often do we take one another for granted?

Here are a 101 ways to provide special attention.

1. Manners - please/thank you	31. Giving 2nd/3rd chances
2. Giving people recognition	32. Understanding people
3. Compliments	33. Seeing their point of view
4. Praise	34. Standing up for people
5. Liking the self	35. Never talking about people
6. Saying yes to life	36. Making them feel special
7. Enjoying people's company	37. Noticing the small things
8. Showing an interest in people	38. Spending time together
9. Listening to people	39. Giving advice
10. Asking questions	40. Sharing knowledge
11. Building rapport	41. Sharing time
12. Flattering people	42. Sharing resources
13. Spending quality time	43. Accepting people
14. Smiling	44. Involving people
15. Open body language	45. Asking for their views
16. Showing understanding	46. Taking time to understand
17. Co-operating	47. Exploring others life
18. Collaborating	48. Sharing experiences
19. Helping people	49. Pushing others
20. Showing people	50. Giving encouragement
21. Laughing with people	51. Being genuine
22. Dreaming with people	52. Really caring
23. Feeling with people	53. Being happy for others
24. Showing empathy	54. Going for win/win
25. Being sincere	55. Making their day
26. Being there	56. Having fun
27. Picking up the phone	57. Laughing together
28. Making the effort	58. Not taking life to seriously
29. Forgiving people	59. Keeping promises
30. Letting go	60. Choosing our attitude

61. Enjoying the moment	82. Saying what you mean
62. Playing	83. Living now
63. Showing interest	84. Exciting people
64. Remembering what they say	85. Being humble
65. Being truthful	86. Being an advocate for life
66. Showing concern	87. Trusting people
67. Focusing on them	88. Trusting life
68. Making the most of each day	89. Thinking big
69. Being your best	90. Working hard
70. Showing integrity	91. Living strong
71. Showing humility	92. Noticing
72. Saying the things that count	93. Appreciating
73. Doing what you say	94. Creating
74. Showing gratitude	95. Dancing
75. Inspiring people	96. Singing
76. Taking action	97. Dreaming
77. Coaching yourself	98. Living
78. Coaching others	99. Loving
79. Being proactive	100. Learning
80. Moving forwards	101. Becoming all you can be.
81. Meaning what you say	

By giving special attention to ourselves and others, we will create positive energy, which will be reinforced to make our life special. The world will conspire to do us good because attitude breeds attitude, behaviour breeds behaviour, and attention breeds attention leading to a positive outcome; a positive world; a life full of energy, vitality and richness through living by our values, the will to love and through special attention.

It is also the ability to do the novel things that stretch us and allow us to take risks and be challenged. To move out of our comfort zone, to positively condition our self by special attention that stretches our capability in pursuit of the Super You.

> *"The ultimate measure of a man is not where he stands in moments of comfort and convenience, but where he stands at times of challenge and controversy." - Dr. Martin Luther King Jr*

To evolve, we need to adapt to new landscapes through new experiences and it is how we respond to those experiences that enables us to be in the fittest shape of our species. It is through self-evolution that we go in search of a positive world in the subterranean landscape of your mind.

'We must cultivate our garden.' - Voltaire

Special attention is the key to success in our life - if we are willing to plan and work on the detail, to go +1 and be inspirational, to work hard and live strong, to be creative and be different, to be proactive and use positive energy, to be a leader and stand out, to challenge the norm and use our freedom to choose - we can be who we want, when we want, whenever we want and the world will help us get there. Trust in life because it trusts in you.

'Use the force Luke' - Obi Wan Kenobi

We have to realize the power we have will enable us to create such a force that we will be surrounded by meaningful coincidences in our life.

Perhaps Schopenhauer was right in that our senses deceive us in that all we can know is our internal world of our thoughts where the body is the appearance of which will is the reality, and our separateness is an illusion, resulting from our subjective apparatus of spatio-temperal perception.

If so, the beauty is, we can create a holistic state of mind in being and create a positive world of becoming in making the most of this life whether it is an illusion of the mind or a voyage of self-discovery.

We become all that we can be through being all that we can become!

A scene from the film 'The Matrix':

Neo is about to meet Morpheus for the first time - he stands outside a room as Trinity opens the door.

Trinity: *"One piece of advice, be honest, he knows more than you can imagine."* Neo enters the room…

Morpheus: *"At last, welcome Neo. As you no doubt have guessed I am Morpheus."*

Neo: *"It's an honour to meet you."*

Morpheus: *"The honour is mine, please sit down."*

Neo sits down nervously....Trinity leaves and the door is closed.

Morpheus: *"I imagine right now you are feeling a bit like Alice tumbling down the rabbit hole?"*

Neo: *"You could say that."*

Morpheus: *"I can see it in your eyes, you have the look of a man who expects what he sees because he is expecting to wake up."*

Morpheus circles the second chair and sits down to face Neo.

Morpheus: *"Ironically this is not far from the truth, do you believe in fate Neo?"*

Neo: *"No."*

Morpheus: *"Why not?"*

Neo: *"I don't like the idea I'm not in control of my life."*

Morpheus: *"I know exactly what you feel. Let me tell you why you are here, you're here because you know something, what you know you can't explain but you feel it - you have felt it your entire life. That there is something wrong in the world and you don't know what it is, but it is there like a splinter in your mind driving you mad. It is this feeling that has brought you to me. Do you know what I am talking about?"*

Neo: *"The Matrix?"*

Morpheus: *"Do you want to know what it is?"*

Neo nods.

Morpheus: *"The matrix is everywhere, it is all around us even now in this very room, you can see it when you look out of the window or when you turn* *on your television, you can feel it when you go to work, when you go to church, when you pay your taxes. It is the world that has been pulled over your eyes to blind you from the truth."*

Neo: *"What truth?"*

Morpheus: *"That you are a slave Neo, like everyone else you where born in to bondage, born in to a prison that you can not see or taste or touch, a prison for your mind. Unfortunately no-one can be told what the matrix is - you have to see it for yourself..."*

He takes out two pills - a red pill and a blue one.

"....This is your last chance - there's no turning back. You take the blue pill, the story ends; you wake up in your bed and believe what you want. You take the red pill, stay in wonderland, and I show you how deep the rabbit hole goes.... remember all I am offering is the truth, nothing more."

Neo takes the red pill.

Ok this is not your last chance, but when you have finished reading this book you can wake up in your bed and believe what you want. You can continue to live in that world pulled over your eyes, the reactive world that has shaped a prison for your mind, or you can find out how deep that rabbit hole goes. It culminates from that feeling like a splinter in your mind, the will to love, your will to love and the feeling to be motivated to become and to be.

It's your choice, you can take the blue pill and everything stays as normal, life goes on, or you take the red pill and stay in wonderland.

A wonderland of positive energy, the will to love, of special attention, a proactive and positive world, in realising who you really are. As stated at the beginning we are all angels; we just need to re-find our wings and fly to our highest hope, your self, the natural you freed from bondage, freed from a world that weighs you down, a free spirit and a deep soul upon the landscape of your life's quest.

Your journey for evermore life.

SPECIAL ATTENTION	EASIEST CHOICE
The Will to love	The Will to nothing
Found	Lost
'I Can' 'I will' 'I love'	'I can't' 'I don't' 'I take'
'I Want to'	'I Have to'
Fulfillment - Yes to life	Emptiness - Life is not fair
Accountable	Victim
Aspiration & Achievement	Aimless
Spirit & Soul	A life of no meaning
Proactive & Positive World	Reactive & Negative World
Whole Person (IQ,PQ,EQ,SQ, PSYQ)	Empty Person
Being & Becoming	Hell on earth

Life Changing Questions

Are you self-evolving?
How do you use special attention to motivate yourself and others?
How can you use special attention to improve your life?
How can you use special attention to please others?
How can you use special attention to motivate others?
How can you use the Motivational Attention Spiral?
How can you use the 101 ways to give special attention?
What world do you choose to live in a dark reactive world or a
    proactive world full of positive energy?

"Life without love is like a tree without blossom and fruit." - Kahlil Gibran

> *And so my friend we near completion in this your world of worlds, what do you choose? What will you become? Where will you go? What will you create? How will you live, love and learn? What corner will you turn? For round that corner a new path awaits into the very soul and spirit of your life…take care my master and live with passion, for tomorrow will be your today and today can be your tomorrow as I help you shape your future history. All my love from the you who knows you best, your higher self who you now know is the Super You who you can choose to be at any time in your life.*

Summary

1. Special attention is the action of the will to love and the end product.

2. Love is all.

3. Special Attention = Improved Performance & Motivation

4. Use the Motivational Attention Spiral to provide attention.

5. The key to success in your life is to use the energy of your will to love and to apply special attention to your own life and others.

6. Special attention creates positive energy through the will to love thyself, others and life.

7. Use the 101 ways to give that special attention.

8. We become all that we can be through being all that we can become!

9. What pill will you choose - the blue pill and return to your comfort zone and life as normal, or the red pill freeing your mind from a reactive life to live in a proactive and positive world?

    If you took the red pill, then welcome to the wonderland of evermore life.

    'When one has once fully entered the realm of love, the world — no matter how imperfect — becomes rich and beautiful, it consists solely of opportunities for love.' - Soren Kierkegaard

Reality Check

1. Chapter 10 focused on inner coaching and the importance of self-coaching to be able to overcome your inner demons through your self talk - this was all about controlling the inner voice by coaching to maintain direction and motivation, as it is your internal dialogue that truly shapes your life.

2. Chapter 11 focused on the process of Characterisation and the realm of becoming, discussing the 3 you's: the Real You, the Blind You and the Super You; and how to use empowerment and enlightenment to become, hence developing Character and Competence through the 3 levels of becoming, the aspirational, motivational and inspirational.

3. The last chapter focused on self-evolution and that through special attention through the will to love you can transform your life. It focused on how to use special attention in all areas of your life to become all you can be.

    Live inspirationally!

    *'What force is more potent than love.' - **Igor Stravinsky***

Interlude 4: The Messiah

"We are all born for love. It is the principle of existence, and its only real end." - Benjamin Disraeli

---

Every day I would awake and start by affirming that I would have the perfect day. Wondering how real my dreams had been, confused by the illusion of dreaming and living wondering if reality really exists.

I felt a ghost upon the landscape observing life afraid and fearful of taking part. Lacking in confidence, too scared to talk.

All the questions were mine with no answers to be found on this planet. A planet I felt was dying through the rape and pillage of mankind.

For man's will to survive and domination is the enigma variation to doom, an unquenchable thirst that releases destruction upon the planet.

In my mind it was only a matter of time as we accelerated towards Doomsday and the ends of the earth. I imagined the Four Riders of the Apocalypse flying across the raging night sky. For each day I would read of war, famine, disease and terror. And I imagined that, even worse than the end itself, was that we knew our last 24 hours had begun and that we only had one more day to live.

So I asked every single person alive what would they do if they had only 24 hours to live? I asked them, what they would do? Who would they spend their time with? What would they value? What would they change? Who would they be for a day? What would they forgive? What would they forget? Where would they go?

And I realized that this would be the perfect day – a day of complete freedom where we act true to ourselves, to our true nature.

For in the moment we are scattered on the fringes of what most consider to be a wasteland where lie all the decay and torment of man's hand.

252

I realized then that both Heaven and Hell do exist on Earth in the minds of the people. I also realized most people are waiting for life to happen (and to end).

And then it happened to me....

Walking across the hill I came across a windmill facing the pool of life, there I was at peace with my soul gazing across the landscape facing an infinity scene of beauty with tears rolling down my face in happiness.

Then he appeared....

For I felt a light bless my face as I came across a man dressed like a king of kings and O how his face felt so familiar. Then he spoke to me with the voice of an angel....

'I have returned to thee my Son of God and I need thee to listen.'

So humbled was I that I fell to my knees.

'O dear Lord.'

'Yes it is I, as foretold he who would return and bring forth the cup of Christ.'

'What would thee have of me Lord?'

'Please walk with me as I have a message for you Saul to take back to the people.'

'Yes my Master.'

'It is time to awaken the people; it is time to return to Eden and for each person to end the waiting. It is time for Heaven on Earth. I have brought the commandments for the next millennium, for thou knows 'thou shall not' for it is built within the soul of the human race.'

'But Master the human race breaks every law.'

'Hmmm, the commandments reinforced negative conditioning in the 'Thou shall not'. Human nature is to explore and learn by experience. In humans' infancy, God's laws were essential to direct the shaping of the world – their purpose was served. Let me begin with the nature of these commandments and how they convey the message of the Lord – this message is 'THOU SHALL' and I have the tablets for you to take with you to the people.'

'O dear Lord, will this change the world?'

'If all human behaviour follows the commandments there will be Heaven on Earth greater than Eden ever was. The sun will shine brighter than ever before and life will be evermore.'

We moved until we came to an observatory and gently sat down. There my Master, my Lord, gave unto me the 10 commandments for the next millennium.

Let me begin.

1. Thou shall live life to the full

   - By taking opportunities

   - By enjoying life at all times

   - By stepping outside of one's comfort zone

   - By experiencing the inner and outer world

   - By leading by example

2. Thou shall give love

   - By giving love freely to develop loving relationships

   - By sharing love to help others

   - By loving the self

   - By loving life

   - By appreciating others love

3. Thou shall become all one can be

   - By having a vision of your ideal self

   - By striving towards your goals and measuring your direction continually

   - By stretching yourself to take the next step to become all you can be

   - By appreciating and celebrating your successes

   - By going the extra mile

4. Thou shall take the good with the bad

   - By learning by experience

   - By appreciating everything good in life

   - By appreciating that all experience is part of the pattern

   - By forgiving those who do you wrong

   - By giving people another chance

5. Thou shall take part and do

   - By taking action without delay

   - By experiencing life each day

   - By realising action speaks louder than words and to do is to love

   - By creating your own tale and being joyful in your own uniqueness

   - By shaping each day through your will to love

6. Thou shall show respect and appreciation of all things

   - By having fascination for all things around

   - By appreciating the present moment

   - By helping others

   - By appreciating the self and your inner qualities

   - By being at one with all things

7. Thou shall continually develop

   - By learning continually

   - By taking opportunities to grow

   - By learning by experience

   - By listening to your inner guide and voice

   - By realising you are part of the pattern and can shape your own destiny

8. Thou shall have self-discipline

   - By staying true to the vision

   - By continually taking action

   - By pushing the boundaries

   - By living with integrity and by your inner values

   - By having the courage to stand up for what you think is right

9. Thou shall smile and laugh in the elation of life

   - By saying yes to life

   - By feeling and being happy

   - By enjoying the present moment

- By sharing humour

- By having fun

10. Thou shall believe in the lord

- By talking to God

- By acknowledging God

- By seeing God in all things

- By finding God's inspiration

- By appreciating there is something as opposed to nothing

The lord gave me the tablets to take with me to the people.

'The time has come Saul for a renaissance of empowerment and enlightenment, a time for the spirit and the soul to live, to love, to learn, to become and to be, to take part in the deep cycle of life for all eternity.'

'Does eternity exist for mankind my Master?'

'In all that you see, hear, smell, taste and touch do you not know the answer to that question? In that case with the fire of your spirit and the depth of your soul I will let you decide!'

Chapter 13: A Sense of Being: The Essence and The Realm

'The universe is transformation; our life is what our thoughts make it' - Marcus Aurelius

---

Before summarising, let's take yet another trip back through time to an epic scene where the prophet Moses flees the Egyptian Army with the Israelites. As Moses stood before the Red Sea they were trapped between the army and the sea, but a miracle happened. God told Moses to lift up his rod and that the waters would part to make a dry path. Moses, a man convinced in his cause with unquestionable belief in his God, parted the sea to the disbelief of his thousands of followers. How could they and the Egyptians not believe in the Hebrew God Yahweh?

Now I'm not questioning whether or not this was God but what if it was actually Moses himself who parted the sea, with such divine belief he could transcend human limitation? Perhaps in a higher state of consciousness where total belief in what a human can achieve, it makes the impossible possible.

The power of belief in our self or others takes us to and beyond the limits of human potential.

The meaning in life is that we believe in something because when we don't life has no meaning.

It is saying yes to life, yes to our self and having our own personal meaning by choosing to believe in that something.

Our life is a gift and we each have a part to play in the pattern – each life is a tale in the making.

There is something and it is that something we have to decide upon and take accountability for – we are responsible.

The key to our success is through our own personal self-talk and inner coaching – for it is that inner voice that we need to control in overcoming our demons and intuitively being aware of our inner guide and quest.

Jung suggested that science has become the main religion of the 20th century replacing religion, and we have lost our attachment to archetypical symbols through our mythology used to provide us with meaning. In the modern day the meaning that gave inner contentment is now replaced by neurosis and personality disorders through a lack of meaning creating a void in people's lives. It is time to re-discover that inner myth in realising we are all part of something and that something can be part of us.

We shape our destiny and our destiny shapes us. It is discovering our inner symbols and feelings for life on a deeper level. We have the freedom to choose our identity, our beliefs and our values. In fact we can choose our own reality because our reality is based on our expectations in life by the life that we choose.

Yes we are creatures of conformity, conditioning and genetic inheritance of which all will have shaped you this far but you have the choice to change and be who you want to be.

If we know what we want in life we can go out and get motivated to achieve what we want. It is generating those feelings and understanding we are motivated by the way we feel about something.

If there were no limitations what would you dare to dream?

With greater belief in yourself what could you achieve?

If you're willing to take risks, how far can you go?

For it is through life experience and the willingness to take part that builds character, that enables us to become our highest hope. Working with a +1 attitude as **aspiration** becomes **understanding** that becomes **enlightenment**, and it is through **action** and accountability that comes your personal **achievement**; truly developing our character and competence – the will and the way.

It is understanding that the reason man is motivated to live is through his will to love himself and others, for the will to love is to take positive action to improve our life and those whom you love. Through the will to love we can work towards the Super You, using our self-talk to coach our self, to have high self-esteem and concept to become all we can be.

In understanding our will to love we realize that it is special attention we give to others and life, which can be the difference that makes the difference. It is living proactively instead of reactively - it is wanting a positive world full of positive energy for our self and others.

As Moses delivered the 10 commandments that gave us the basic laws and also conditioned us 'Thou shall not', the next millennium is about 'I Can' and 'Thou Shall'. If you were to take the 10 commandments from the last Interlude, the Messiah, and score yourself out of 10 (10 being perfect), what aspects of your life can you improve and change?

Life is all about 'Being and Becoming' and everything we have discussed has been aimed at **Becoming** all you can be.

You can be your highest hope.

So where do we go now if we understand the workings of our ideal self, our highest hope, the Super You? We have the goals and aims in line with our principles and values. We are saying Yes to Life and we are willing to take part.

But with everything in life we don't want to go too far one way because the green eyed Devil of Becoming can be 'I want', 'I want', 'I want'. Our direction is lost through the materialistic dragon of shallowness that leads us to a life of greed, although I would stress this should never happen if we are consistent in our aim of the Super You and how the Super You would act.

But it is here that I would like to turn to the Essence of Being.

In life it is essential to have a balance between Being and Becoming. If all life was Becoming, we would never really stop to appreciate the moment and if all life was Being, then it would just pass us by.

So what is being?

There are different states of Being:

1. **Who are we Being?** This is the state of being in the sense it is who we are being when we are doing what we do and know in life. This is the person we choose to be and the state is the mood, condition, and behaviour we display. If we choose to be proactive then we can control who we are being all of the time.

    In life it is who you are being when you are becoming all you can be that matters and makes the biggest difference!

    Don't let life dictate who you are being by living reactively.

2. **Being all we can become.** This builds on choosing our state of being by choosing who we want to be when we are the Super You, i.e. if the Super You would be energetic, happy and fun then it is acting and being like that right now.

3. **Sense of Being.** This is the sense of being one with all things; it is that feeling of being in the present moment, the contentment of the spirit and the wholeness of the soul.

4. **Ultimate Being.** This builds on the last point with those transcendental moments of inspiration. The being one with a higher spirit or the sense of illumination through a beautiful experience.

5. **Outer Body Being.** The higher states of consciousness awake, or alternatively, in dreams; the feeling of exaltation through the leaving of the body.

So why is being so important? Being is the appreciation of the present moment and timeless moments; it is autogenic conditioning of the mind in being oneself, all things and the inner contentment of the moment to be oneself. It is also the appreciation that in that present moment everything becomes timeless – universal soul and in some respect universal understanding. It is the glimpses of the greater pattern and the path to illumination.

Let me stress being is not a process like becoming is – it is the essence of being – it is a feeling and cannot be touched.

THE ESSENCE OF BEING

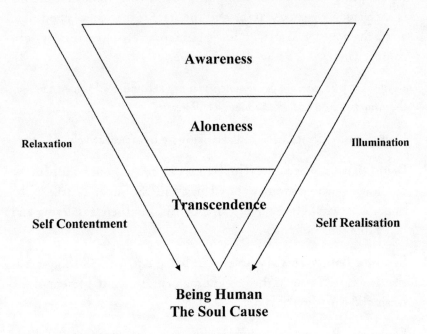

Awareness is the realisation that through meditation and relaxation that one can control one's thoughts taking over one's mind. It is the emptying of the mind to feel the sense of oneself in the present moment.

Aloneness is that sense of being comfortable with oneself – it is the appreciation that we are all alone and it is that sense of being that is not afraid or living in fear, it is the trust to let life happen and believe in the flow and circle of life.

Transcendence is that higher sense of being one with nature, all things and ultimate being, the soul cause and soul eventuality.

It is essential that we find our sense and essence of being through choosing who we are being and giving our self time to meditate and relax in being our self in the present moment; having those moments that are free from becoming to simply be.

So we strive to become all we can be and it is being all that we can become. It is finding that balance is the mystery of life with the fire of our spirit and the depth of our soul within the essence and the realm.

> Listen to the Exhortation of the Dawn!
> Look to this Day!
> For it is Life, the very Life of Life.
> In its brief course lie all the
> Verities and Realities of your Existence.
> The Bliss of Growth,
> The Glory of Action,
> The Splendor of Beauty;
> For Yesterday is but a Dream,
> And To-morrow is only a Vision;
> But To-day well lived makes
> Every Yesterday a Dream of Happiness,
> And every Tomorrow a Vision of Hope.
> Look well therefore to this Day!
> Such is the Salutation of the Dawn!
> - Kalidasa

In combining the process of becoming and the essence of being we live our life as a fully integrated individual where the soul guides the spirit and the spirit guides the soul. Through the process of Becoming we develop self-character and self-competence through aspirational, motivational and inspirational goals. This is through the empowerment of the Real You and the Enlightenment of the Blind You to work towards the Super You. In contrast, the Essence of Being we find self-contentment and self-realisation through relaxation and illumination on a personal awareness, appreciation and acceptance of aloneness and by finding a higher state of being in transcendence. This is driven by the will to love, through being and becoming and developing on a psychological, physical, mental, emotional and spiritual level.

Being & Becoming
Human Dynamics

Becoming the Super You
(The Fire of your Spirit)

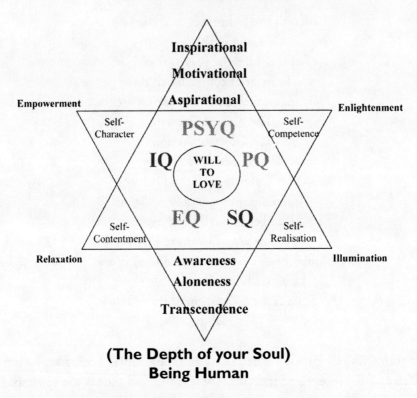

Inspirational

Motivational

Aspirational

Empowerment   Enlightenment

Self-Character   PSYQ   Self-Competence

IQ   WILL TO LOVE   PQ

EQ   SQ

Self-Contentment   Self-Realisation

Relaxation   Illumination

Awareness

Aloneness

Transcendence

(The Depth of your Soul)
Being Human

The Soul Cause and the Soul Eventuality

What we do in life (and who we are being) echoes for all eternity!
- Maximus (Gladiator)

Interlude 5: The Magician

"Though we travel the world over to find the beautiful, we must carry it with us or we find it not." - Ralph Waldo Emerson

The Presenter (or is it the Magician to me?) and the Dialogue

"Welcome back. I hope you have enjoyed today's conference. What were the key lessons for you? How can you change your world? Change your life? How can you feel the fire of your spirit and the depth of your soul? How can you lead a more complete life? I wonder....

So let's sum up then, what is human dynamics? The art of becoming all you can be and being all you can become - is it that simple?

Life offers you choices and with every choice will come a benefit and a consequence but the beauty of life is that you are free to choose.

Now let me take you back to the tale of those two very different men at the start. One had lost everything, his family and his way in life. He lived like the world owed him something and he lived selfishly through taking everything for himself leaving a destructive trail as he blazed across the landscape. The second man chose to give and to live in a proactive and positive world believing the world conspired to do him good. His glass was full to the brim in his saying yes to life, living by his principles and values in line with his deep inner quest in life.

Which man do you choose to be?

And what if I were to tell you that both men were in fact the same man faced with the same choices as you, just as all men through the ages have been faced with the same choices? You can choose to go left or right, take the blue pill or the red pill, the choice is yours. What does your conscience tell you? What is your purpose?

Do you choose to be in control of your life or have it control you?

Do you choose to live reactively or proactively?

Together we can change the world but first you have to choose to change your life, yourself and fulfil your destiny.

So..... *One can be master and win*

Or serve and lose

Grieve or triumph

Be the anvil or the hammer,

What are you my friend, the anvil or the hammer?"

(The reactive or the proactive?)

Epilogue: Evermore

"The meaning of life is that it stops." - Franz Kafka

To end I return to that fateful day, April 15th 1989, and Hillsborough, April 15th, the same date that the Titanic sank, another tragedy, different year. I think of all the catastrophic tragedies that have happened lately: September 11th, the Twin Towers in New York; the Tsunami in Asia; the Hurricane Katrina laying waste to New Orleans; the First and Second World Wars; any war of recent; all tragedies. The simple point I am making is you can never really appreciate what a disaster is like unless you were there, and you were part of it. With Frankl and the Nazi concentration camps we can only begin to imagine the terror the Jews experienced and through films like Schindler's List along with books we can only begin to feel the terror.

So I return to Hillsborough because for a young man to actually wish he were dead through the guilt of being alive but then to realize that he had been given such a gift to be alive is an experience in itself. The only way I could put things into perspective was kind of like this...

I am 18 years old - what if I never returned? I imagined my Dad waiting on the corner alone in his fear; I imagined the total despair he was in and then the total grief as I did not return. I watched how it affected his life, a broken man cursing himself through guilt, blaming himself as his life fell apart. I watched how it affected my Mother, her collapsing on the news of her son's death, the loss of her eldest son, her baby. I watched the different life they would have led without me, the pain, and the torture as they rebuilt their life. How it affected my brother and sister and closer friends and family.

An empty world, so totally unfair in its prescription.

A completely different script and the ripples of negativity that would have spread across so many lives, a tale of sadness not in my end but in everyone else's life who lived to be affected by such a sorrow. A sorrow that could possibly have caused pain, illness, distress, envy, desperation, destruction, despair, anger, separation by carrying such negative energy from such a loss.

It was only through this that I could even begin to understand the pain; the terror and the horror that the families who lost loved ones must have felt and how it possibly affected them.

What it made me realize is that we are given the gift of life for as long as we are here and we should make the most of that life in a positive way – anyone who has left this world would want this for you. We should try to make a difference in this world starting by making a difference to ourselves and how we think. We can choose to be a victim or we can become accountable to make a difference in life. We are all unique and we all have a part to play in the pattern. The 96 shall never be forgotten and they never died in vain but lived perhaps to die so that no such a disaster could ever happen again. The magic of Liverpool is (in my belief) that they are still there watching their beloved team at Anfield in spirit and will be re-united with their loved ones in good time.

It also made me realize that we will never truly understand life.

Humanity's Sorrow

If a man was placed before an infinite scene of beauty in happiness he would cry tears of an eternal sadness.

Life is about choices, it's about a test of faith. It's about appreciation for the present moment and living in that present moment. We are free spirits, both you and me, able to choose the paths we take, and through that gift of life we have a chance to decide what to do with the something given to us.

So through your will to love, trust in life and the something you have, more importantly trust and believe in yourself.

I challenge you....

To see the light and not the dark
    To find solutions and not problems
To feel joy and not despair
    To listen to your inner coach and not your inner critical demon
To live proactively not reactively
    To search and live in a positive world not a negative one

If we all go in search of a positive world we can make this life, this world, this place, this moment, and every future present moment, all it can be.

It is better to have loved and lost than never to have loved at all.

It is better to have taken part than to have not taken part at all.

Even in the face of adversity I would cry and shout to the ends of the earth,

'To live, to love, to learn, to become all you can be and be all you can become.'

Let the human spirit fly....

Evermore

Shade, spirit and dream
Across the darkening void
Through the planes unseen,
Startled, alive on the verge of death,
Discovery beyond the waking dead.
Past gravestone, tomb and horror,
The midnight air breathing
Wanton disarray of madness.

Sorrow, sadness and threats
Apart from high ideals ill kept,
To times of unparalleled sight

That keeps the dark abyss alight,
Treasures found, secrets told,
Beyond the gate made out of gold,
A place of riches, a dreaming door,
In that this path leads to Evermore.

O Evermore, O Evermore
Upon the glades of Evermore,
As ever shall or ever will
The course of life does ever spill
Upon this tale of living.
Through darkened days and less travelled ways
Lies speculation as to where the present be,
Past eternity's shores and infinity's falls
To a land of misplaced identity,
A broken morality.

Demon, incantation and hell,
Illusion, damnation and spell,
The nightmare realm of sleep.
Awake, as round the corner waits
New adventures and promised fates,
Threads upon the wheel of turning
Through experience and in the learning
As legends do surely weep.

Cloud, rain, and fall,
From natures beckoning call,
To everybody on morning breeze
Rivers of blood filled cities,
Structures of the wildest sorts
Built upon our lovely thoughts,
To enlighten you and enlighten me
Gathering all to simply be.

One Evermore.

O Evermore, O Evermore
Upon the plains of Evermore,
As ever was or ever can,
The story of the evolving man,
In endless depth and sincerity.

Ancestors of old and parables untold,
For what is the price of a human soul,
A wanderer's hope, a jester's joke,
The valleys graced with heavens folk,
The running stream, the child's dream,
History told and all that's been
Right down to the road where it all began,
The universe's inscrutable plan.

A raven's wings, a blackbird sings,
Of all things, of all things,
A baby cries, an old man sighs,
For the hope of where forever lies,
A midnight kiss, a state of bliss,
The bizarre feeling all is amiss,
Along the path to the eagles nest
Is where one finds the travellers rest.
There in time and there in space
Within the spirit finds true grace,
All one was and all one seems
Is all one dream, is all one dream,
Leading on towards old oaks door
And the golden land of Evermore.

O Evermore, O Evermore
The dreaming place called Evermore
With ever wishes and ever days,
Where true love finds its ways
Above the force of entropy.

Chamber, lust and storm,
Through a changing world undone.
Forever as one all things
Living to the point that danger brings,
Visions of unholy lands
Where no one truly understands,
Upon a changing darkling plain
Where nothing ever stays the same.

Dreams, happiness and fun
Beyond the sun where it all begun,
To shadow realms below above
Of lost love, of lost love.
Left to carry the burning flames,
Fire alive where it never rains,
Feelings one can never change
Forever the love of another strange.

Across new paths and never ending laughs
One finds one's place where the present be,
Here today but gone tomorrow
A searching for harmony.

A search for the soul, a search for the self,
Where lies the true meaning of mankind's wealth?
A mild intervention, a cruel wait,
For how can one escape this forsaken fate?
Taking one to disarray, taking one aboard,
Taking one to the steps of our dear Lord,
Crying to the people, crying to the place
Entwined within the threads of the human race,
Shaped by a sculptor and sculpted wrought
Where lands are broken by battles fought,
Across the dimensions of the cosmic core
Where hope lies within the place called Evermore.

O Evermore, O Evermore,
O Evermore life.

A tale in the making, a time one sings,
Of all things, of all things,
Of all things, of all things,
Truly evermore life one sings.

O Evermore, O Evermore,
O Evermore me,
O Evermore, O Evermore,
O Evermore free,

Evermore.

Your time is now...

Finally I leave you with a taste of *'Being & Becoming - In Search of Forever'* as I will be asking, what would motivate man to live forever?

Bibliography

Motivation & Personality by Abraham Maslow, Longman.

Towards a Psychology of Being by Abraham Maslow, John Wiley & Sons.

The Essential Plato by Alain de Botton, TSP Publishing.

The Individual Psychology of Alfred Adler, Harper Perennial Books.

Unlimited Power by Anthony Robbins, Pocket Books.

Awaken the Giant Within by Anthony Robbins, Pocket Books.

Get the Edge by Anthony Robbins, Robbins Research International.

Introducing Aristotle by Rupert Woodfin and Judy Groves, Icon Books.

Ethics by Aristotle, Penguin Classics.

The World as Will and Idea by Arthur Schopenheaur, The Everyman Library.

Transitions: The Challenge of Change by Barrie Hopson, Mike Scally, Kevin Stafford, Mercury Business Books.

A History of Western Philosophy by Bertrand Russell, Unwin paperbacks.

The Great Philosophers by Brian Magee, BBC Books.

The Story of Philosophy by Brian Magee, DK Limited.

Maximum Achievement by Brian Tracy, Fireside Simon & Schuster.

Memories, Dreams, Reflections by Carl Gustav Jung, Flamingo published by Fontana Paperback.

Modern Man in Search of a Soul by Carl Gustav Jung, New York: Harcourt Brace.

Man and His Symbols by Carl Gustav Jung, New York: Laurelleaf.

The Origin of the Species by Charles Darwin, Penguin Classics.

On Death & Dying by Elizabeth Kubler Ross, Simon & Schuster.

On Grief & Grieving: Finding a Meaning of Grief through Five Stages of Loss by Elizabeth Kubler Ross & David Kessler, Simon & Schuster.

Thus Spoke Zarathustra by Friedrich Nietzsche, Penguin Classics.

Beyond Good and Evil by Friedrich Nietzsche, Penguin Classics.

Human all too Human by Freidrich Nietzsche, The Cambridge Edition.

Motivation to Work by Herzberg, Transaction Publishers.

Critique of Pure Reason by Immanuel Kant, The Cambridge Edition.

Mindstore by Jack Black, Thorsons.

The Mythic Tarot by Juliet Sharma-Burke & Liz Greene, Guild Publishing London.

A Theory of Cognitive Dissonance by Leon Festinger, Evanston.

Nietzsche, Philosopher, Psychologist, Antichrist by Kaufman, Princeton.

Learned Optimism by Martin Seligmen New York Alfred A. Knopf.

The Road Less Travelled by M.Scott Peck, Arrow.

Philosophy 100 Essential Thinkers by Philip Stokes, Capella.

The Monk Who Sold His Ferrari by Robin Sharma, Element.

The Interpretation of Dreams by Sigmund Freud, Penguin Classics.

Beyond the Pleasure Principle by Sigmund Freud, W.W. Norton & Company.

The 7 Habits of Highly Effective People by Stephen R Covey, Simon & Schuster.

In Search of Excellence by Tom Peters & Robert H. Waterman Jnr, Harper Collins Business.

In Search of Meaning by Viktor Frankl, Washington Square Press.

The Will to Meaning by Viktor Frankl, Meridean.

Work & Motivation by Vroom, Jossey Bass Wiley.

Useful Websites

http://www.businessballs.com/

http://chiron.valdosta.edu/whuitt/col/motivation/motivate.html

http://www.quoteland.com/topic.asp?CATEGORY_ID=232

http://www.robinsharma.com/ic_home.php

http://www.completeperformance.co.uk/

http://www.itsnlp.com/index.htm

http://www.motivatingquotes.com/

http://www.empoweringmessages.com/

http://www.slyasafox.com/book/book_1.html

http://www.franklincoveyeurope.com/

http://www.anthonyrobbins.com/Home/Intro.aspx

http://www.queste-qld.com/

Special Thanks

To my Wife for putting up with my quest and lack of
special attention especially when I have been locked away
writing or as she would say *'Making another list.'*
I Love You.
To my Mum & Dad for giving everything and expecting nothing back
in return: My Mother has taught me values of honesty, decency, and
truth as well as a little about organization (I mean a lot) and strength
of character. My Father has taught me how to forgive and be generous,
genuine and happy. Both have taught me not to get upset by the little
things…*'Paul, it's not really important when you look at the bigger picture..'*
I Love you both.
To Lynn McLeod for all you help and wisdom, but
even more so for editing this rollercoaster ride, you are
a true friend and purple sage for all seasons.

Readers Feedback

Can you please send feedback through to
apositiveworld@aol.com
to let me know what you thought of Being & Becoming
Finally Make the most of every moment because if you don't I will!
Many Thanks
Paul Corke

LaVergne, TN USA
15 August 2010

193335LV00002B/200/A